BREAKTHROUGH

CRPVK.

After leaving school at the age of sixteen to work as an office junior, Margaret L. Flanders built herself a successful career in management, breaking through her own glass ceiling to become a strategic planner in a multinational industry. At the age of 40 she set up her own training and consultancy business, providing specialist services for women and for the self-employed. She is the author of several articles on business management and career development; Vice-Chair of the London East TEC Community Advisory Board; Management Committee Member of New Ways to Work, The Women Returners' Network and the Women At Work Network; Liaison Officer for OwnBase and a Business Advisor with the Prince's Youth Business Trust. She has been married and divorced, and now lives with her common-law spouse. She has no children and one cat.

BREAKTHROUGH

The career woman's guide to shattering the glass ceiling

Margaret L. Flanders

Paul Chapman
Publishing Ltd

Paul Chapman Publishing Ltd
144 Liverpool Road
London
N1 1LA

British Library Cataloguing in Publication Data

Flanders, Margaret
  Breakthrough: Career Woman's Guide to
  Shattering the Glass Ceiling
  I. Title
  658.40082

  ISBN 1 85396 233 3

Typeset by Inforum, Rowlands Castle, Hants
Printed and bound by Athenaeum Press, Newcastle upon Tyne

A B C D E F G H   9 8 7 6 5 4

CONTENTS

INTRODUCTION

What is the glass ceiling – Purpose of this book – How to use it

We are facing a plastic ceiling – if it were glass it would have shattered by now. We just need to keep hammering away at it.

(Barbara Mills, Director of Public Prosecutions)

WHAT IS THE GLASS CEILING?

The phrase 'glass ceiling' sums up all the frustrations of working women at every level who can see where they want to get to but who find themselves blocked by an invisible barrier. The attitudes of society generally, group or individual prejudice, restrictive male-based working practices, lack of the support available to men through their old boy network – these and many more factors conspire to build and strengthen the barriers around and above us.

> While it seems relatively easy for women to gain employment at the lower levels of organizations, it is still proving very difficult for them to reach upper, middle and senior management positions, even in the more enlightened USA.
>
> (Davidson and Cooper, 1992, p. 13)

We may encounter the glass ceiling several times in the course of our working life. The move from clerical/secretarial/supervisory level to junior management has always been the hardest career step for both men and women, followed by progression from middle to senior management and then senior management to board level. Not all of us aspire to such heights but no matter what our aspirations, we all, of whatever sex, race, religion, age or physical or mental ability, deserve the chance to progress as high as our capabilities and aspirations allow. Being prevented from doing so, whether by deliberate acts, by the attitudes of society generally, or by individual circumstances is an infringement of our basic rights as members of the human race.

PURPOSE OF THIS BOOK

This book has been written for every woman who wants to change or control her circumstances in order to achieve full satisfaction in her working life. Much academic research has been done into the causes of women's career problems and I have not repeated that which has been published elsewhere, other than by referring to it for background information. Instead, by talking to women of every working level and recording their experiences and advice, and by analysing my own experiences gained during more than twenty years in management and latterly in running my own business, I have produced a practical guide which will enable you, the reader, to recognise your own personal glass ceiling and take the necessary steps to avoid being trapped beneath it.

There is no magic formula for success and reading this book will not change your life overnight. By highlighting the problems faced by other women, giving you examples of how they coped – or in some cases didn't cope – and by encouraging you to think objectively about your own situation, I intend this book to be the catalyst which will enable you to create your own success.

HOW TO USE IT

Each chapter is broken down into sections covering specific issues with discussion about the issues, case studies to illustrate them, practical exercises for you to carry out in your own time and tips for coping with the topics covered. You need not work through the book in chronological order – each chapter is headed with a summary of the issues covered and you may prefer to turn directly to those which are of the most immediate interest. However, I recommend that you also familiarise yourself with the topics covered in other chapters, in case you should face any of these issues yourself in the future.

Case studies

All the case studies are taken from real-life situations. Wherever possible I have identified the woman who experienced that situation but some have requested that I withhold their name to protect their privacy and in these cases I have used a fictitious first name.

Initially you may be unable to identify with some of the case studies, in that the circumstances are not ones which you expect to face or where the woman concerned was at a different stage in her career. Rather than skipping over that case study and the questions and tips relating to it, you will find it useful to first analyse the situation objectively to see whether you can think of any alternative action that she could have taken, and then picture yourself in a similar situation so you can think how you would have coped. This will help you should you ever have to face such a problem yourself in the future.

Tips

The tips in each section have been compiled from the experiences of all who contributed to this book.

During my researches I came across many useful sayings put forward by women. These are far too valuable to keep to myself so I have used these within the text in the hope that they will stimulate you when you find the going hard.

Further information

Information on useful publications and organizations is listed in this section at the back of the book. Details were correct as at the date of publication.

1

RECOGNISING THE GLASS CEILING

Traditional working patterns – Attitudes and prejudice – Isolation and lack of role models – Exclusion from the 'old boy' network – Training – Being seen by men as a threat – The culture trap and the way we think and act – The effects of recession – Summary of causes – Recognising potential barriers

> The main difficulty I have with my colleagues is that it's not that they don't want women, it's that they don't know them. People appoint people they know – if you don't meet them, they don't get to know you. You need to try to make time to network, get involved, get known.
>
> Baroness Jean Denton

Few of us regularly take time out to think objectively about our career. It is only when we encounter problems or see others getting ahead before us that we begin to wonder what is wrong, and often this is too late for us to put things right without a lot of heartbreak and stress. By understanding the causes of the glass ceiling and learning to recognise typical situations before we find ourselves in them, we can take preventative steps to avoid many of the pitfalls.

There are many different and sometimes inter-related causes of the glass ceiling. This chapter summarises them and provides pointers on recognising the situations which are likely to cause problems.

TRADITIONAL WORKING PATTERNS

The traditional working pattern of education–full-time career–retirement is based on the typical working lives of men. There is no such single typical working pattern for modern women, yet society continues to try to force us to conform with the traditional stereotype for male workers. If we cannot conform, many employers are reluctant to employ us in positions which have previously been filled by men.

> Working time is structured in radically different ways for women and for men. Put at its simplest, the time men spend in paid employment determines how much time they have for their families: the time

women spend caring for their families determines how much time they have for paid employment. As a result, the pattern of women's working lifetimes, as well as the organization of their working time over the week and the year, are very different from those of men.

(Hewitt, 1993, p. 4)

This is of course not true in all cases – many women choose to put their career before, or equal to, their families – but it does illustrate one of the major differences between working women and working men.

There are several different working patterns for women which vary depending on personal circumstances and ethnic origin, including:

- continuous full-time work with no career break
- continuous full-time work interrupted by short maternity break(s)
- full-time work leading to part-time work following maternity break
- full-time work with lengthy maternity break, followed by return to either full- or part-time work in later life
- continuous full-time work leading to part-time work in later life to care for elderly relatives
- full-time or part-time work interrupted by spells of unemployment due to lack of jobs
- full- or part-time work carried out from home
- self-employment.

Women are therefore far more likely than men to require a job which allows them flexibility. Career breaks to have children or look after elderly relatives are an inevitable part of many working women's lives and at long last some employers are coming to terms with our need for flexibility by introducing formal career break and family-friendly working arrangements such as term-time working, jobshare, and flexitime. Regrettably, many managers continue to assume that not only is a woman's prime role that of a wife and mother but also that women prefer this to be the case. The widespread assumption is that women are far less committed to work and far less able to undertake a full-time career than men, and when it comes to promotion, given a choice between a man and a woman with equal qualifications, the employer will frequently view the woman as the greater risk. Typical attitudes are:

When it comes to promotion and career development, women are judged not so much on their abilities and achievements, but on assumptions about their family life, responsibilities and future intentions.

'Men are treated as workers, not parents; but women are always seen as mothers.'

(Spencer Stuart & Associates Ltd, 1993, p. 4)

Employment law, trade union attitudes and social security rules all serve to support and perpetuate the traditional male working pattern. Until these are radically changed, many women will continue to have no option but to juggle with work and family responsibilities, often to the detriment of their career.

Practical exercise: Working Patterns

(1) Identify the working pattern which relates to you.
(2) Consider objectively the effect your working pattern has had on your career to date.
(3) Consider the effect your future working pattern is likely to have on your future career.
(4) List up the changes in either your personal circumstances or your employer's attitudes that would help you to satisfactorily progress your career.
(5) To which do you give the highest priority – your working life or your personal life?

TIPS

- If your personal circumstances prevent you from following the career you would really like, you may need to reassess either your priorities or your career plans. Be prepared to have to compromise to obtain the balance which best suits you.
- Consider actively looking for a career or an employer which offers more flexible working arrangements.

ATTITUDES AND PREJUDICE

We all use our past experiences to help us decide how we should act now and in the future. As well as being human nature, this is good management practice, but only so long as we carefully evaluate whether or not the lessons learned from our past experiences are fully valid in the current situation. There is a serious danger of stereotyping when we fail to ensure that the people we are currently dealing with actually will act in the same way as those we dealt with in the past. The stereotyping of women by employers is one of the major causes of women's career problems.

> Men discriminate against women by making assumptions about an individual woman, based on their limited experience and general stereotypes . . . Because women are assumed to be less committed to their careers than men, it is also assumed that they are unwilling to make the sacrifices and adjustments necessary to advance their careers. If a woman manager is married, it is assumed that she would not be interested in jobs that provide real challenge and development, if such jobs also entail relocation or long periods away from home.
>
> (Spencer Stuart & Associates Ltd, 1993, pp. 5–6)

The assumption that women are unwilling/unable to commit themselves fully to their employer is only one of many. Other such assumptions are that:

- the flexible working patterns required/preferred by many women run counter to the requirements of the company
- women lack the leadership qualities needed to successfully head up a team or organization
- women dislike power, or are afraid to handle it
- women are generally less assertive than men and will avoid confrontation wherever possible
- women lack the ruthlessness necessary for success in a competitive market
- women are only better than men in the 'caring' fields of work such as teaching or personnel
- the male managerial style is the only acceptable one.

Discrimination on grounds of sex is illegal. However, until these deeply rooted emotional and cultural attitudes can be changed, women will continue to be seen as 'second-best'.

For ethnic minority women, discrimination is an even greater problem, again frequently arising from prejudice and stereotyping. Disabled women face additional barriers – the physical constraints imposed on them by working conditions designed for the more able-bodied plus an element of 'fear', arising from managers' and colleagues' lack of understanding and reluctance to discuss disabilities objectively in case they cause offence.

Practical exercise: Attitudes and Prejudice

(1) What are the attitudes of your co-workers – do they treat you the same as your male colleagues? If not, in what ways do they treat you differently?

(2) What attitude does your boss take towards you? Does this differ from the way in which your boss treats your male peers?

(3) Do you treat your female colleagues and staff in the same way as males? (Be honest with yourself!)

(4) Do you prejudge any of your working contacts on the basis of their sex, race or physical ability? Are your assumptions actually valid? (Be honest with yourself!)

(5) What action can you take to dispel the prejudices and change the attitudes of others in their dealings with you?

TIPS
- If you find you are being prejudged incorrectly, try to ascertain whether the person concerned is stereotyping you because of a previous personal experience, and if so, consider what action you can take to make them realise that you are different.
- Consider whether your own attitude and behaviour might be reinforcing their attitudes.

ISOLATION AND LACK OF ROLE MODELS

The vast majority of employers, board members and senior managers in the UK are male. Women who do make it through to the top find themselves isolated and lacking female support amongst their peers. To safeguard their own position they often have to either themselves adopt male attitudes or go along with the majority and are thus unable by themselves to introduce the changes in working practices and attitudes that are needed to enable other women to reach senior level.

This situation is gradually improving as an increasing number of women opt for a full-time career and make it through to the top, but it is a long slow progress. Senior women have little time to act as mentors to their juniors, and sadly many are reluctant to risk compromising their own position by championing women's issues, though as the number of senior women grows, more are becoming active campaigners to help increase the opportunities available to the rest of us. This lack of role models does nothing to help women at lower levels – we have difficulty in seeing first-hand how senior women conduct themselves and few examples to cite to employers when trying to convince them that women are at least as good as men.

EXCLUSION FROM THE 'OLD BOY' NETWORK

For many women, mixing socially with male colleagues in after-work hours is not a practical proposition. Family commitments combined with the possible safety risk of travelling alone late at night may deter us from socialising in the evenings. Also, it is not unusual for women to feel uncomfortable when mixing with an all-male group, particularly when the discussions turn to predominantly male interests such as sport, or when the men's attitude becomes avuncular or sex-orientated.

> I tried socialising with my male colleagues after work but found that instead of them treating me as they do during working hours, their attitude became one of 'looking after the little woman'. They were reluctant to let me buy a round and frequently apologised for their language and jokes. Instead of helping me to increase my rapport with them, I felt awkward and as if I was there on sufferance. I now very rarely go to the pub with them.

Isolation from the old boy network may come from either the impracticability of socialising after hours or from the attitudes of the men themselves, with the result that many of us are unable to take advantage of this opportunity to build up good relationships with our colleagues on a social level and to learn from the grapevine. Although there are now a wide number of women's networks, these are of little help when we need to increase our rapport with our male colleagues.

TRAINING

Although many women hold higher academic qualifications than their male peers, women in employment generally receive less training than men. Employer attitudes discriminate against women by assuming that money spent on training them will not be well invested; many courses are held at locations or times unsuitable for part-timers and working mothers, and women themselves often do not make a point of requesting training. This creates problems when women are seeking promotion, because their employer views them as being less well-skilled than their male counterparts.

BEING SEEN BY MEN AS A THREAT

Those women who have already made it to the top often did so because their male peers did not realise what was happening. Now that those women have publicly proved themselves, men have become aware of our capabilities and ambitions and many are starting to see women as a real threat in the career stakes and are actively taking steps to safeguard their own chances.

Such steps may range from deliberate perpetuation of stereotyping or male-orientated working practices to subconscious or active discrimination. The men who most fear us are usually those with lesser ability or confidence, but if they are part of the 'old boy' network they are often in a position to damage our prospects.

THE CULTURE TRAP AND THE WAY WE THINK AND ACT

Stop being your own worst enemy and start being your own best friend.

Those of us born in the 1940s, 1950s, and even the 1960s to some extent, were conditioned in our early years by sex-role learning. At school, girls were automatically taught cookery and needlework and opportunities for learning 'boy's skills' such as carpentry or science subjects were only available to the very few. Many of us had mothers who gave up work on getting married or when expecting their first child and parents and careers teachers who assumed we would do the same in due course.

Our early conditioning creates an attitude of mind (the 'culture trap') which is difficult to change as we become adult. Thus, many women have low expectations and a low view of their abilities and become afraid to take on tasks traditionally allocated to men or which involve a degree of power. Until the majority of individuals change their thinking, society as a whole will continue to believe in the traditional male/female role segregation.

Therefore, not only must we recognise and fight the external barriers caused by society, traditional working practices and male attitudes and prejudice, but we must also question the values and assumptions that we may have learned in early life and examine our own attitudes in order to recognise the barriers which we ourselves help to erect and maintain. Unless we change the way in which we both think and act, our own attitudes and actions will continue to reinforce the stereotyped image of working women.

> I have been told by friends on a number of occasions 'this is typical, you are putting yourself down again. Why do you keep doing it?'

The changes we need to make include:

- objectively identifying our skills and personal attributes, concentrating on these rather than on our failures
- challenging our own assumptions about women's roles
- learning to believe in ourselves and raising our personal expectations
- being clear as to how we can best combine our working and personal life
- being clear as to the image we wish to project to others
- setting ourselves higher goals to aim for
- making the most of every opportunity to take on challenging roles
- speaking up instead of allowing others to speak for us
- not being scared of success
- taking pride in our achievements and maximising rather than minimising our successes when discussing them with others
- actively seeking better training and higher qualifications, where necessary for progressing our career
- learning to recognise barriers and prejudice and how we can best surmount these to enable us to achieve our full potential.

Until we accept full responsibility for our own lives and see ourselves as fully accountable to ourselves, we will continue to act in a way which merely reinforces the attitudes and prejudices against working women.

THE EFFECTS OF RECESSION

The recession of the early 1990s resulting in a serious reduction in the number of available jobs has created an additional barrier. Many employees have been forced into redundancy thus more people are chasing fewer jobs, and statistics show that more women than men have remained out of work or have accepted a position at a lower level than their capabilities in order just to stay in employment. Women looking to return to work after a career break are at an even greater disadvantage. Even though the economy is now picking up, it is unlikely that employment will in the foreseeable future reach the peak of the 1980s – those companies that have survived have found not only that hiring and firing comes expensive when redundancy payments are involved, but have also learned to streamline their processes and make do with fewer employees. The coming 'demographic timebomb' was a familiar phrase a few years ago, but the recent reduction in the overall number of jobs means that we no longer have this to look forward to as the complete solution to our problems.

It is not our fault that women have been far harder hit by the recession than men. Employment is a buyer's market, with the result that we stand less chance than men of regaining employment because:

- men seeking employment at middle and senior management level tend to have greater continuous employment experience than women
- employers continue to view women as a higher employment risk than men
- employers frequently still view men, rather than women, as the main breadwinner and therefore subconsciously feel that men have a greater need to work.

Sadly, women are again being turned into second-class citizens in the employment stakes.

One improvement which has taken place during the recession is the increase in women taking up self-employment. This may stem from a lack of any viable alternative as much as from personal desire; nevertheless, it is an encouraging sign both of women's determination and commitment, and our capability.

SUMMARY OF CAUSES

- traditional working patterns, upheld by employment law and trade union attitudes, which are more suited to men than women
- the dual family/work responsibilities of women which give rise to discontinuous employment and the need for more flexible working patterns
- deep-seated attitudes and prejudices against women, resulting in stereotyping and misconceptions, with even greater prejudice against ethnic minority and disabled women
- lack of training in management and personal skills
- the increasing isolation and lack of peer support as women progress up the ladder
- the lack of role models
- exclusion from the old boy network
- conscious or unconscious discrimination from men who see us as a threat to their own career
- the culture trap, women's own attitudes and lack of belief in themselves
- a severe reduction in the number of available jobs due to the recession of the early 1990s

RECOGNISING POTENTIAL BARRIERS

Be Prepared – motto of the Guide movement.

Recognising potential problems in advance enables us to take action to prevent them arising or to minimise their effect. Many of us have jobs which involve identifying potential problems and planning solutions, yet few of us take the same advance action when it comes to our career so it is no wonder that we suddenly find ourselves with limited prospects for advancement.

Case study

Angela (not her real name) is an administrator in a medium-sized independent organization with extensive national influence in the technical field, several UK sites and a high international profile. She is a graduate, has been in post for three years and has shared supervisory responsibility for one of her section's secretaries. She would like promotion but vacancies are few and far between and most specify technical qualifications. She applies for vacancies when they arise and has reached the interview stage for three out of the five vacancies which have arisen since she joined the organization, but without success. The majority of managers in her organization are men and most hold technical or professional qualifications though not necessarily ones relevant to their posts. After one unsuccessful interview, Angela was told she was not appointed because she lacked in-depth technical knowledge – a fact which should have been apparent to the selection panel from her initial application.

Although when she first joined the organization it appeared to be one which would offer her a reasonable chance of advancement, it is currently undergoing a re-structuring and re-grading exercise and is shortly to start a large-scale relocation exercise which will make Angela's daily journey even longer than at present. It has no formal career planning or mentoring procedures and the annual appraisal system has been suspended until the re-structuring has been completed. Her boss recently left and her group is currently managed on a temporary basis by the boss of the other half of her section – he will be coming up for retirement in a few months, following which her section will be taken over by an existing male manager who will give up his current section in order to take on both halves of hers.

Angela found her former Personnel Manager (a woman) quite approachable but was told by a colleague that it was not the done thing in this organization for someone of Angela's level to approach the Personnel Manager direct. Her managers are now all middle-aged men and she gets no support from her female colleagues, most of whom openly declare that they are 'looking after number one' and some of whom actively undermine Angela's authority over the section secretaries, making it impossible for her to maintain the discipline and standards she feels are needed.

Angela finds her present work lacks challenge and would welcome an opportunity for both increased responsibility and increased international travel, but is unsure as to the field of work her qualifications and experience would most suit her for. She finds it particularly unfair that her employers expect relevant qualifications from women and take no account of their transferable skills, yet promote men whose qualifications do not specifically relate to the job. She holds a number of committee positions outside work from which she gets far greater recognition and appreciation than she does from her paid job, and considered studying for an MBA but decided this would be of little immediate help in advancing her career. Although she has been applying for other jobs and has been interviewed for one, she finds it difficult to undertake a concerted job-search campaign because of the practicality of combining this with her full-time work in an open-plan office, her long daily commuting journey and her committee responsibilities.

Recognising that she is getting 'nowhere fast' with her present employer, she now plans to concentrate her efforts on finding other employment, even if this means resigning before she finds a new job.

Questions:

(1)   What barriers is Angela suffering from?
(2)   Is there any action she could have taken over the previous few years to improve her promotion prospects?
(3)   How highly do you rate the chance of her improving her job satisfaction and promotion prospects within this company?
(4)   What action can she take to increase her chances of finding a new job?

Recognising potential barriers before they arise involves:

−   thinking objectively on a regular basis about your current situation and your ambitions
−   identifying and recognising the culture of your current employer and the attitudes of management towards women employees
−   understanding the likely causes of career barriers and identifying those to which you might become vulnerable
−   being aware of the image you project and how your colleagues and bosses view you
−   being aware of your colleagues' performance – the image they project and the progress they are making compared with your own.

Practical exercise: Identifying potential barriers

(1) When did you last think objectively about your career, identifying where you want to get to and by when?
(2) When did you last think objectively about your colleagues, their performance, image and achievements compared to your own?
(3) How aware were you (before reading this chapter) of the potential barriers to your advancement?
(4) What is the prevalent culture and attitudes towards women within your present company?
(5) What are your own attitudes and expectations? Are you suffering in any way from the culture trap; do your own attitudes and actions reinforce traditional views about working women?
(6) Re-read the list of barriers and make a note of those which you feel you currently face/may face in the near future. Add in any additional barriers which may relate to your own particular circumstances.
(7) For each of the barriers, try to identify the people/situations/circumstances which are likely to cause them.

Keep this list for reference as you read through subsequent chapters.

2

WOMEN IN ORGANIZATIONS

*Where women are employed – How the glass ceiling affects employers
– Organizational structures and cultures – Women in clerical and
secretarial roles – Women as supervisors – Women in management –
Managing yourself and your work – Women at board level*

What really matters is changing the culture of the organization.
(Joanna Foster, former Chair, Equal Opportunities Commission)

You cannot decide on the best way to demolish the barriers you face or
may encounter in the future without first understanding both your position within your organization and also how you fit into the particular
field of work or working pattern you have chosen or in which you currently find yourself.

There are many different types of employer, with a variety of organizational structures and cultures in a wide range of fields of work. Some
barriers may arise because your way of thinking and working does not
accord with that of your employer, or because you are failing to keep
yourself informed about the trends and developments which affect the
future direction of your company. Others may be due to your having
chosen a field of work deemed to be non-traditional for women and
therefore not geared to widescale female employment.

The glass ceiling is usually taken as referring to problems faced by women
at management level. However, women encounter barriers at all levels of
their career, be they on the first rung of the ladder or in sight of the top. It is
useful to think about the causes of barriers for women at lower levels to you
so you can help your own sub-management staff and to ensure that you, as
their manager, are not unconsciously helping create their barriers.

WHERE WOMEN ARE EMPLOYED

Although women make up nearly half the UK workforce, the majority of
us work in low status occupations or in a limited selection of business
sectors. Over 60 per cent of working women are found in clerical and
related industries (with women filling the majority of typing, secretarial

and cashier posts); in education and training, health and welfare and public administration; and in catering, cleaning and other personal services. The banking and finance sector has traditionally been a large employer of women, as is the Civil Service with almost half of their employees being female. One theory why the public sector attracts more women is that they have traditionally done more to recruit women by offering them equal employment terms and flexible working practices; however, even in these areas, women still dominate the lower grades and only a small proportion are found at higher levels.

At middle and senior management and at board level, the proportion of women falls even more drastically and improvements are only seen in those few organizations which have made a positive effort to increase the number of women at senior levels. Some 80 per cent of clerical workers and 97 per cent of secretaries are female and women still only account for 3 per cent of senior managers and 9 per cent of management as a whole. However, about half a million women return to the workforce each year, and labour market trends show that women are expected to account for just over 80 per cent of the labour force growth by the year 2006 (Employment Department statistics).

Although 25 per cent of the UK workforce now works part-time, the majority of these are women (47 per cent of all women and 50 per cent of women over 35 years old, as opposed to 12 per cent of men). Part-time working is itself a barrier to promotion, with many employers refusing to consider that more senior jobs can be done on a part-time basis. Only 3 per cent of women managers currently work part time; few part-time women employees receive training, thus making it even more difficult for them to gain promotion.

Despite increased efforts throughout the last decade to encourage women to enter the more non-traditional fields of employment, there are still only a very few of us to be found in industries such as engineering, technology, physical sciences, architecture and building. Not only do we have to overcome our own early conditioning and lack of opportunities for gaining a technical education, but often the recruitment and training procedures pose additional barriers, such as the wording of advertisements, physical and mental selection tests designed specifically for male abilities and concepts, training geared to a predominantly male workforce, and lack of role models.

The picture therefore is one of women making up nearly half the workforce but being found predominantly in specific fields of work, with a comparatively low level of responsibility (and thus working for comparatively low pay), and with almost half of us working part-time.

HOW THE GLASS CEILING AFFECTS EMPLOYERS

It is not just the individual who suffers because of the glass ceiling. Employers who do little to encourage women into higher positions are seriously restricting the resources and the diversity of skills and experience which could be available to them, by failing to make the best use of existing female employees, or because women who feel they are not being given a fair chance soon start looking for an alternative employer. Employers who make no suitable provision for retaining women after maternity leave waste time and money on recruitment and the cost of training replacement employees. Companies unprepared to offer flexible working practices restrict the number of women recruits they attract. There are also the hidden costs relating to public opinion, where more enlightened members of the public or investors may seek to restrict their dealings with companies seen as less than sympathetic to the employment needs of women.

Looking to the future, the reducing numbers of young people who will be entering the job market over the next decade will force employers to make better use of their existing workforce's potential and to recruit from those groups which have in the past been ignored, such as women, older workers, ethnic minorities and people with disabilities. Those employers who do not already have the required culture and working practices in place will find difficulty in attracting workers from these groups, thus adversely affecting their potential efficiency, productivity and profitability.

ORGANIZATIONAL STRUCTURES AND CULTURES

Growing international competition, the widespread use of new technology and increasing pressure for greater emphasis on quality and customer care have resulted in radical changes in the workplace. The traditional organizational structure, based on a strict hierarchy whereby responsibility/authority and promotion was in an upwards direction only, is giving way to the 'flat' structure. Employers are realising that change is a feature of growth and that without flexibility and constant change business will stagnate and companies will lose their competitive edge. Staff numbers have been reduced to create a leaner, more flexible organization with fewer management levels, fewer functional boundaries and a greater emphasis on project management and teamworking.

The management skills needed in a 'flat' organization are very different to those required in a traditional hierarchy. Employers need multiskilled staff who:

- can react quickly to change
- are willing to work with less rigid job boundaries
- keep their existing skills up to date and are willing to learn new ones
- are willing and able to take on greater responsibility
- understand the implications and practical uses of technological advances.

Unfortunately, employers are failing in the way they instigate these changes. Many have implemented wholesale restructuring and dramatic reduction of management levels without having given their employees the information and the skills they need to cope with the change. This leads to misunderstandings, confusion and fear of redundancy, causing stress, low morale and loss of employee loyalty. The more ambitious and perceptive employees who are keen to see both themselves and their company be successful suffer considerable frustration and often either seek a new employer or give up the battle – either way, the employer loses out. An example of this is found in the teaching profession, where constant changes in the educational system have led many teachers to resign and seek a different career. I have many times over the last few years heard it said that 'those with the get-up-and-go got up and went'!

Understanding the structure and culture of your organization is vital to your career prospects. If your company culture is one of judging employees by the amount of time they spend at work rather than on the results they achieve, views women as predominantly low-grade material with low ability and low aspirations, provides little or no training and career planning for women, and is reluctant to introduce family-friendly working practices, your career prospects could be seriously affected.

The attitudes and culture of a company depend to a great extent on both its size and the business sector it is in. Companies in the private sector are motivated by market forces and their need for profit, whereas those in the public sector, although now adopting the departmental cost-centre concept, are motivated more by the need to adhere to rules and regulations laid down for them. A large organization is likely to have clearly specified individual posts and a defined career structure; employees in a smaller business often have no clearly defined responsibilities and no formal career structure. These fundamental differences affect both the type of employee attracted to the company and the culture and attitudes found within it. Often, people moving to a different company-type have great difficulty in understanding and relating to the culture they find themselves faced with, because it is different to anything they have previously experienced.

Practical exercise: How well do you understand your organization?

(1) Does your organization have a 'flat' or 'hierarchical' structure? How many management layers are there? Has this changed radically in the last few years?

(2) Does it have a Vision and Mission Statement, and written short-, medium- and long-term Objectives? Do you know what these are, and do you understand them?

(3) Is it at the mercy of central political decisions? How does this affect your career prospects?

(4) Do you know what your company's position is in the market-place and what market forces and trends are likely to affect it in the future?

(5) How is change managed in your organization? Are employees given adequate information about the reasons for the need to change? Are you consulted or invited to become involved in major decisions and in planning

or implementing changes to structure and management practices? Do you and your colleagues feel fired with enthusiasm for such changes, or do you feel apprehensive, under-valued, frustrated and demotivated?

(6)   Are employees actively encouraged to put forward new ideas, act on their own initiative, liaise with colleagues in other departments/fields of work/in different grades?

(7)   Are employees actively encouraged and helped to improve/extend their skills? Is your company a member of the Investors in People campaign?

(8)   Does your organization have a system of career planning for each of its employees?

(9)   What percentage of overall employees are female? Which jobs do the majority of them occupy? What percentage of managers are women? Are women actively encouraged to seek promotion?

(10)   Does your organization have any declared policy towards the employment of women? Does it provide family-friendly working practices such as flexible working? Is it a member of the Opportunity 2000 campaign?

(11)   Do the attitudes of your bosses and colleagues towards you as a female employee bear any relationship to your organization's policy on the employment of women? (i.e. if you feel the fact that you are female is preventing you from progressing your career, is this because the culture of the company as a whole is less woman-friendly than it could be, or because of the attitude of certain individuals?)

(12)   Do you find your colleagues being promoted solely on the basis of their abilities, or is there a strong element of 'it's not what you know, it's who you know'? How much bearing do internal politics have on your promotion prospects? Are you in a position to get to know the people that matter, or is this an opportunity others have but which is denied to you?

See Tips on page 20.

WOMEN IN CLERICAL AND SECRETARIAL ROLES

Clerical and secretarial employment represents over 17 per cent of the UK workforce with the majority of jobs being filled by women, many of whom have low or no qualifications. Because these posts have traditionally been filled by women, many employers assume that women have low career aspirations, but a study carried out for the Employment Department (Henley Management College) (1992) found that clerical workers are keen to develop their skills, requesting training beyond the on-the-job, informal type – for example National Vocational Qualifications (NVQs). And several surveys have found that secretaries rate challenge, responsibility and job involvement as more important than money.

Typical barriers facing women at these levels include:

– employers' assumptions that:

    – women do not want responsibility and challenge, promotion or a full career

---

TIPS: Understanding your organization

- If you are unsure where to start with these questions or find the prospect of thinking about them daunting, try to find a colleague to work through them with you.
- If you don't know the answer to several of the questions, is this because this information is not made freely available to employees, or is it because you have not previously taken an interest in such matters?
- Now ask yourself what sort of picture you are getting about your employer:
  - Does it seem as though the company knows where it is going and what it wants to achieve?
  - Is it subject to external forces which prevent it from having clear future goals and achieving these?
  - Is it making the best use of its human resources in structured or innovative ways, or is it just 'muddling along'?
  - Is it woman-friendly, or is the potential of its female employees mostly overlooked?
  - Do the promotion prospects of employees depend more on 'playing the game' and 'it's not what you know but who you know' than they do on the ability of individuals?
- Discuss the picture you are getting with a colleague. Do they get the same picture, or is your perception different to theirs? Does the perception of female colleagues differ to that of male colleagues?
- Finally, ask yourself whether you feel comfortable with the picture you now have of your organization. If you feel uncomfortable and can see no likelihood of your picture changing, it is probable that you are working in the wrong organization and will either have to come to terms with accepting the culture as it stands and learn to make it work for you, or think seriously about moving to a different employer.

- women lack the skills and qualities required by management
- younger women will soon want to give up work to have a family, so that training or promoting them would be a waste of company money
- women give priority to their family over work and thus prefer routine jobs that leave them with the time and energy they need for their family
- women with family commitments are not prepared to work outside normal hours or undertake company travel
- higher-grade jobs can only be carried out by full-time workers
- older workers are entrenched in their ways and cannot be taught new skills

- lack of:

  - a formal career structure leading to management positions
  - training provision for lower-grade and/or part-time workers

- a boss who feels you are so good at your current job that to promote you and thus have to find a replacement would reduce the efficiency of the company.

Secretarial work is generally felt to be of higher status than clerical work, as secretaries combine mechanical tasks such as typing with more social tasks such as administration, liaison and providing support to the boss on an *ad hoc* basis. But the status of the secretary is tied to that of her boss, and opportunities for secretarial workers to gain promotion or move into other areas of work are fairly limited. Personal Assistant posts provide slightly higher responsibility and sometimes lead to a supervisory or junior management role.

CHECKLIST FOR ACTION

Managers and secretaries can take the following action to increase involvement and ensure the best use of a secretary's abilities.

Managers can:

- work with their teams to establish work practices which minimise unnecessary typing and clashes in priorities
- ensure their secretary is included in departmental meetings and establish regular work-related discussions to inform and involve
- include their secretary in the organization's appraisal and induction processes, and set realistic, achievable targets in order to provide challenge and growth
- identify career opportunities for their secretaries, and communicate these.

Secretaries can:

- discuss areas of their manager's work which can be delegated, in order to vary and enlarge their job and save management time
- define their training needs and be prepared to justify them to their organisations in terms of the benefits to them, to their managers and to the organization as a whole
- ask the questions that will keep them informed and put forward the ideas that will make them and their teams more effective.

(Hepburn, 1991), reproduced with permission from The Industrial Society

Many sub-management positions are in small companies where the number of total employees limits promotion opportunities within that company. Even in bigger companies, clerical and secretarial posts are often not integrated into mainstream career structures, training for higher-level work is not provided and managers do little to encourage women to seek promotion. The part-time nature of many of these jobs is an additional barrier, as few employers are prepared to offer part-time posts at a higher level.

Clerical and secretarial skills are readily transferable, making it comparatively easy to move to a different employer, though in the short term the individual may gain few advantages apart from perhaps slightly higher pay or more convenient working hours or location. Given that labour market trends report employers finding difficulty in recruiting and retaining administrative and secretarial staff, hopefully employers will eventually be forced to offer benefits such as improved training and promotion prospects in order to attract the employees they need.

To obtain a more senior position, you may need to specialise in a particular type of company or field of work, or undertake general management training to expand your skills.

TIPS

To be successful at these levels and improve your chances of promotion from a sub-management position:

- Ensure you are giving out the right 'signals' – i.e. that you are not reinforcing your employer's assumptions about women and their attitude to work.
- Ensure your boss knows about your ambitions and that, despite your loyalty to your existing employer, you would seriously consider moving to another company if that is the only way to progress your career.
- Keep your skills, particularly computing and interpersonal skills, fully up to date – be prepared to have to arrange your own training if your employer will not provide this.
- Discuss with your boss your career prospects, current skills and abilities, and any additional skills that you need to obtain. Aim to get agreement to a structured plan for advancing yourself.
- Ensure you have the skills needed for higher-level work – you may have to undertake study or training to gain these.
- Consider specialising in working in a particular type of industry, such as becoming a legal secretary, so as to have something extra to offer an employer.
- Read advertisements for job vacancies to find which fields of work are in greatest demand and consider studying for one of these fields or taking training, such as an NVQ in Business Administration or Management, for more general higher-level work.
- When seeking employment/alternative employment, ask the employer what training and career development facilities are provided, letting them know you are keen to progress beyond your existing level. Try not to take employment with a company which offers little prospect of advancement.
- Don't under-rate your existing skills and experience – clerical and secretarial skills are an excellent grounding for higher-level work and are often of more immediate practical use to an employer than academic qualifications based on theoretical study.

WOMEN AS SUPERVISORS

The role of the supervisor is changing. According to a report from the Advisory, Conciliation and Arbitration Service, supervisors will be taking increased responsibility for the recruitment, assessment and training of staff. The report also forecasts that leadership skills will become as important as the traditional technical skills. With the growth of work groups which allocate work among themselves, the supervisor's strength will lie more and more in being able to motivate colleagues, which in turn means that supervisors will increasingly need to be seen as part of the management team. They must have a clear role within an organization and be given adequate induction and training, particularly in management skills.

(Employment Department, 1992)

This is encouraging for women, who are widely seen as being better than men in 'people skills', but to progress to the next level, women supervisors must make it clear to their boss that they would welcome becoming more involved in managerial decisions and being given the opportunity to obtain management skills. Supervisory responsibilities which can be directly developed into management skills include:

- technical leadership and competence with new technology
- the organization and management of work allocation, processes and systems, time, staff and financial resources
- quality control
- recruiting, managing, motivating, training, developing and appraising staff
- communicating and teambuilding
- personnel, disciplinary and industrial relations matters
- health and safety.

If you are in a supervisory post, do you take personal responsibility for all the above? If not, can you gradually expand your duties, or get your boss to agree to your expanding them, to cover all aspects? Do you highlight all these skills in your CV?

If you are the manager of supervisory staff, do you allow them to take responsibility for all of the above, and if not, why not? By allowing and encouraging them to take on all these responsibilities, you will free up more of your own time thus enabling you to concentrate on those tasks which will help you improve your own career prospects.

WOMEN IN MANAGEMENT

It is widely believed that men and women exhibit different styles of management. Whereas male managers are highly competitive, liking to be seen as the decision-maker and thus often reluctant to discuss issues with their colleagues and staff because this could be seen to be 'weak', women actively instigate discussions with those involved in order to reach a consensus decision, thus avoiding confrontation by the use of persuasion and compromise. This has given rise to the assumption that women lack the leadership qualities required to successfully drive a team or organization.

Women are also thought to be generally less assertive than men in promoting themselves or their views, and therefore lacking in the ruthless qualities that are considered to be needed by top management. Spencer Stuart (1993, p. 11) quote the following typical statements made about women managers:

"If you take 100 women, 80 may be fantastic Number 2s; if you take 100 men, only 50 are likely to be fantastic Number 2s, but 50 may be good Number 1s."

"Women don't let ego get in the way. Which is why they make good Number 2s. They are terribly good at getting the boss's orders understood and accepted."

"Women will always look for consensus while men try to divide and rule. A woman will say 'These are the ways we can solve the problem: how many people can we get to agree with it?' A man says 'This is the way we are going to do it, and if you don't like it, you can resign.'"

This stereotyping ignores the fact that we are all individuals, with individual approaches to managing our work and our staff. As Spencer Stuart (1993, pp. 11–12) point out:

Certainly, women and men behave very differently in some instances. But will this remain the case as women become more confident and comfortable in positions of authority? And more to the point, do these differences indicate some sort of inferiority?

"I think it is a matter of style, rather than substance. We all develop our own style of leadership and, over the years, we come to recognise the different styles of leadership that our male colleagues adopt. Women must do this as well, but we are just not familiar with their styles."

The real question here is not whether women have traditional leadership qualities, but rather whether such qualities are relevant in today's culturally diverse, complex organizations.

We can use at least some stereotyping to our advantage here. The particular qualities that women are popularly renowned for are precisely those needed by today's 'flat' organization, e.g.:

- flexibility, adaptability and ability to react quickly to change
- able to handle uncertainty and surprise
- aware of ethics and values, and a balanced perspective
- project management, team leadership and good 'people' skills
- multiskilled managers willing to work within less-rigid job boundaries.

Again, quoting from Spencer Stuart (1993, p. 12):

"A good team player is someone who listens and who respects others. My experience is that women make better team players than men."

"What, after all, is management? Managing resources. And women are very good at that."

"We have to get away from this 'do as you are told' style of leadership. It is not relevant to the way our businesses are developing. And it is not the way to develop intelligent managers."

> **TIPS**
>
> - Identify those skills and abilities needed at the level above you and look for specific examples to illustrate that you have those skills.
> - Make sure your boss is kept fully aware of your skills and achievements. In particular, stress those abilities traditionally associated with women (such as interpersonal skills, team leadership, persuasion, etc.) and take every opportunity to illustrate how your employer can benefit from these – thus making stereotyping work for you, not against you.
> - Use your teambuilding abilities to set up co-ordinating groups with other departments or companies so your strengths get known to a wider audience.

We all need to find ways in which we can have an impact.
(Stephanie Monk, Confederation of British Industries)

The role of the manager

Without a clear picture of your current function and the wider responsibilities of management in general, you will find it difficult to convince others that you have the skills to take on a more demanding role. The pressures of day-to-day responsibilities allow little time to regularly sit back and consider our management techniques, but it is vital that we ensure we are not creating barriers for ourselves because of a lack of appropriate skills and qualities. Information on the many different management styles and techniques abounds and the study of this can be fascinating or boring, depending on your outlook. As numerous books on how to improve your skills are published each year and are widely available, I do not intend to look in depth at every single skill that successful managers require. Instead, I have concentrated on those areas which my research shows are of most immediate concern to women.

MANAGING YOURSELF AND YOUR WORK

You will only manage your work effectively if you are able to manage yourself.

Managing your emotions

Our emotions inevitably have an effect on our behaviour. Without emotion, we would be less than human and would be unable to develop rapport and understanding with the people around us. The marketing slogan 'selling is nine-tenths the transfer of enthusiasm' is a good example – an emotionalless salesperson is unlikely to be much of a success. We need to understand our emotions and the way in which they affect our behaviour, so that we can make them work for us, instead of against us.

TIPS

- If you make a serious mistake, face up to it, take whatever steps you can to correct it, learn from your mistake and then concentrate on the positive aspects of the future. Don't try to cover it up; avoid becoming defensive, looking for excuses or putting the blame on others. Don't waste time and energy brooding over it – you can't change the past but you can influence your future.
- Face up to your fear of failure and then take steps to minimise the chance of it happening:
  - visualise the worst possible outcome, objectively assess the chances of it happening and then ask yourself 'so what?' (i.e. how serious an effect would it really have on your prospects?) Once you have faced up to the worst possible outcome and start to think objectively about how you would cope with it, you will be able to make more rational and less emotional decisions and the magnitude of the problem will begin to reduce
  - be realistic about the likelihood of failing: ask yourself what is the most *likely* outcome (as opposed to the worst possible outcome)
  - decide on the ideal outcome you would like to achieve, then plan how you can achieve this. Be as objective as possible – treat this exercise as you would a practical work problem rather than a personal one
  - don't allow your fear of failure to become self-fulfilling – instead of constantly thinking about failure, concentrate on thinking about the ways in which you can achieve success.
- Accept that nobody is perfect and that there is nothing wrong in making a mistake, provided you learn from that mistake and take steps not to repeat it in the future.
- Don't assume that others' criticisms of you are always justified – seek a second opinion.
- Don't assume that just because things have gone wrong in the past they will do so again – the fact that they did go wrong before actually means you are more likely to avoid making the same mistake again. Concentrate on thinking positively – visualise yourself being successful and then plan the steps you need to take to achieve this.
- Concentrate on your strengths and achievements rather than your weaknesses; remember that both men and women regularly under-achieve their potential – don't let this happen to you.
- Remember that success requires a sustained effort and a certain degree of failure along the way. If you know and understand yourself, have defined goals towards which you are continuously striving, and believe in your abilities, you will succeed.

Self-doubt is the most destructive of human emotions. It makes us question our own judgement, reduces our productivity because we do each job several times over to ensure we have made no mistakes; makes us afraid to attempt anything new or take even the smallest risk, and causes mental stress which in turn affects our health. The most common causes of self-doubt are:

- making a serious mistake

tranquilliser

out of control.

- fear of failure
- believing that to be successful it is necessary for us to be perfect in everything we do, thus setting ourself standards which are impossible to achieve and our fear of failure becomes self-fulfilling
- believing that when others criticise us, their opinion is always the correct one
- negative thinking – assuming that because things went wrong for us in the past they will do so again in the future.

Women are often cited as thinking more about their weaknesses than their strengths. In studies of recruitment, women have been found to avoid applying for jobs where they feel they cannot match the required criteria 100 per cent, whereas men were found to focus on the criteria they could meet, not letting the fact that they lacked some of the requirements prevent them from applying. It is important not to totally ignore our weaknesses otherwise we will never know we need to improve them, but concentrating on our strengths and achievements helps us build up confidence and self-esteem and enables us to become a better manager.

Loss of self-control leads to anger and aggression or a feeling of hopelessness and depression, but it is not easy to always keep our emotions under control. Loss of control can be caused by frustration at events beyond our control, having to deal with difficult people, problems in our personal life or because our physical health is not 100 per cent perfect.

When my boss told me my contract was not being renewed, my stomach started knotting and I felt sick. It was a toss-up as to whether I burst into tears or jumped up and hit him – my whole world seemed to have shattered and I felt a complete failure.

TIPS

- Learn to recognise the factors that affect your capacity for self-control, such as high levels of pressure, people with a particular personality type, disappointment, the state of your physical health.
- Plan in advance the best way to handle such situations, so you are prepared if your temper begins to rise or you start feeling weepy.
- If you feel yourself losing control, take several deep breaths and concentrate on calming yourself down. If possible, try to defer the situation until later when you have had a chance to regain control.
- Concentrate on making your emotions work for you instead of against you, by channelling the adrenalin released by strong emotions into positive, rather than negative, thoughts and action.

I kept finding myself reacting irrationally to situations at work, getting worked up for no apparent reason and feeling that I couldn't cope with the pressure. I lost my temper over silly little things or wanted to burst into tears if anyone said anything even slightly critical to me. It was only after I talked this over with a friend that I realised I was suffering from premenstrual tension, which was making me exaggerate every little problem. Once I realised the cause, I found I could cope quite easily, because I was prepared for it to happen.

I particularly detest men who make comments about women's menstrual problems, such as publicly citing this as the cause of what they (the men) deem to be emotional or irrational behaviour in females. If the comments are general, I find it best just to ignore them. If they are addressed to me, I say calmly 'Actually, that was last week, and it's not something I suffer from, anyway'.

There will always be times when things get too much for us and we just want to crumble. Crying is a safety valve which helps relieve the immediate pressure, but it is best to do this in private or with a close friend if possible. Don't feel bad or guilty about crying – instead, think how much better off we are than men, whose macho image prevents them from making use of this safety valve. However, *do* avoid using tears in public as a means of getting your own way!

Be organized and know your priorities

You cannot be properly organized unless you know what you are meant to be doing and can judge what is important and what is trivial. All good organizations have written Value and Mission Statements and set themselves short-, medium- and long-term Objectives. As a manager, you should do the same thing, preferably as a joint exercise with the colleagues in your team, to help you prioritise your work and focus on the important tasks.

Setting yourself similar personal statements will help you to judge what is important and what is not in terms of your career plans.

Manage your time

Good time management takes practice. By planning what needs to be done, setting yourself deadlines by which to complete each task, monitoring your progress to ensure that you meet each deadline, and identifying 'time thieves' such as unexpected telephone calls, staff interrupting you with trivial questions, time lost in chatting, etc., you can minimise time wastage and will become a more effective manager. Excuses used for not managing time include:

- 'There's not enough time to plan and monitor – I just have to jump in and get on with the work.' If you don't properly plan your work, how can you be sure that you are using your time in the most effective way?
- 'I feel it is important that I am available to talk to my staff whenever they want my help.' Do your staff really need to rely on your help all the time? How do they cope when you are at a meeting or on holiday? Are they asking for your advice so as to save themselves the bother of having to make their own decisions?

We cannot actually manage time – it exists independently of us. What we need to manage is ourselves and our tasks. If your personal priority on a particular day is to get home early because of a family commitment, organize your day round this priority and be firm when circumstances or people try to steal your time.

Be seen to be in control

A cluttered desk is *not* a sign of genius – it is usually viewed by others as a sign of a cluttered mind! If you look efficient and effective, cultivate a calm, collected manner in front of others, and save the screaming and shouting until you are somewhere private, you will give the impression of being in control of both yourself and your work.

Don't let yourself be panicked by circumstances or other people. Be sure that you know to whom you need to be accountable – your employer/ yourself/your peers etc. – and be clear about what it is that you are accountable for, so that you can decide on your priorities. Remember that other people's priorities will often be different from yours – don't rush to fulfil their priorities without first mentally checking to ensure that this will not jeopardise your own. Learn to say 'no', when it is appropriate.

Keep yourself informed

Pressure and lack of time make it is very tempting to concentrate only on those matters which affect our current job. Being viewed as an expert in your own field is not enough. If you don't keep yourself informed about wider issues such as general company policy, developments in other departments, national and international opinions and trends, you will seriously restrict your promotion opportunities.

Use your travelling time to catch up on your general reading, consider making one of your staff responsible for looking at all the general company information that comes your way and summarising this for you on a weekly basis.

Practical exercise: How well do you manage yourself and your work?

(1) How many times in the last year have you let your emotions affect your judgement? What can you do to prevent this happening in the future?

(2) How often do you mentally list up all your achievements and successes? Do you think about these more often than you think about your failures?

(3) How often do you organize your work, draw up a list of priorities, and monitor your performance against your objectives?

(4) How often do you allow other people's priorities to take precedence over your own?

(5) How often do you spend longer than you should on a piece of work because you worry that you might have made a mistake somewhere?

(6) How much time do you waste in a day on unimportant things, and how much of your time do you allow others to 'steal'?

(7)   Do your attitudes, actions and working space announce to others that you are fully in control?
(8)   Do you create pressure and stress for yourself and your staff by not being able to say no?
(9)   Do you keep yourself as up to date as you should do about matters of general interest?

Many women executives say they have to work a lot harder than men to be successful, citing a variety of reasons for this:

My male colleagues and boss don't take me seriously as a manager, so I have to make sure my work is 100 per cent correct at all times to show that I am as good as them.

Because I can't afford to make mistakes which will damage my credibility, I find myself doing tasks which I know I should really delegate to my staff. I have to come in early nearly every day to get through my workload.

It is expected in my company that managers work longer than their contracted hours. If I go home earlier than my colleagues, they accuse me of slacking.

In order to prove myself, I started volunteering for special high-profile projects. I enjoyed the challenge and the recognition this gave me, but it put me under tremendous pressure because I still had my regular work to complete as well. When it got to the point that all the extra work was automatically given to me, I began to realise that I was being taken advantage of. I am now very careful about which projects I take on and have found that turning work down has actually made others respect me more.

I used to feel I had to work twice as hard as my male colleagues in order to prove I was as good as them. Now I realise that it was myself I was trying to convince – my lack of self-confidence had made me feel that my performance was being put under the microscope, when in fact I was being treated no differently to anyone else.

Practical exercise: Do you feel you have to prove yourself?

(1)   Do you frequently work longer than your contracted hours?
(2)   Do you work longer, shorter or the same hours on average as your male peers?
(3)   How often do you do work which you should really delegate to your staff?
(4)   Do you feel you have to work harder than others in order to prove yourself?

WOMEN AT BOARD LEVEL

Modern thinking states that the format of a board of directors should represent the format of that company's customer base. To quote Spencer Stuart (1993, p. 13):

TIPS

If you feel that you have to make more of an effort than men in order to prove your competence, ask yourself:

- Is it really others I need to convince, or is it myself?
- Could I delegate more effectively?
- Am I actually being inefficient by trying to make sure that all my work is 100 per cent perfect?

The New Mythology has also created the idea that 'a woman's point of view' is essentially different from a man's point of view and that, especially in companies selling products to women, the female point of view must be represented at Board level.

In many cases, this leads to the appointment of a 'token' woman on the board. None of us want to be appointed as a gesture instead of for our abilities, but it is a start on which we can build. Once we are appointed to the board, we can use our influence to get additional women appointed, but we must be prepared in the meantime to cope with the problems of isolation. The number of women being appointed to boards is gradually increasing but it will still take many years to achieve full equal representation of both sexes, partly because of the deep-seated attitudes of existing male board members and partly because of the lack of women at senior levels with the required skills and experience.

One way to increase women's representation is for more of us to take up appointments as non-executive directors – although such positions are mainly voluntary, they do allow us to actively demonstrate our capabilities.

Case study

Maggie Williams, Organizer for the East Sussex Association for the Disabled, was appointed as a non-executive director of the Sussex Training and Enterprise Council (TEC) in 1991 when that TEC was first being set up. She was approached by the board chairman who was looking for non-executive directors living in East Sussex with an interest in special needs and who could represent the voluntary sector – he did not know Maggie personally but she had been recommended to him as meeting the required criteria.

Maggie felt the position would be a good learning experience for her and would also benefit her organization. Initially she found it rather intimidating because she was the only female board member, was given no guidance as to board procedures or her responsibilities and had to learn a whole new field of business. The other directors (mainly white, middle-class older men) were very polite and gentlemanly towards her but she found they had preconceived attitudes about the voluntary sector, believing it was made up of out-and-out campaigners or members of the 'blue rinse and pearls' brigade, and they had little experience of special needs – being hearing-impaired herself gave Maggie an ideal opportunity to educate her fellow directors. A further problem was the lack of remuneration – being employed by a charity, Maggie lacked the high salary level and support services enjoyed by her fellow directors and had to spend around one day a week of her own time, often at weekends, on board work.

> It took me about a year to get to grips with the procedures, learn about the TEC's field of work, get to understand the people and their sub-agendas and earn their respect so that I could work on educating them and changing their attitudes. I initially spent a lot of time listening carefully to what they said but saying little myself – once they realised that I was not a threat and they began to understand the voluntary sector better, they started listening to me.

Maggie's tips include:

- believe in yourself and don't allow yourself to be intimidated
- listen carefully
- make what you say count
- work on earning your colleagues' respect and educating them in a non-confrontational way
- remind your male colleagues that equal opportunities issues are the responsibility of everyone, not just women
- suggest that the board sets aside time for 'getting to know you' sessions – every so often, Sussex TEC holds a board dinner after the meeting or directors take a day out somewhere to work together on a particular issue
- use your appointment as an opportunity to increase your own skills and knowledge as well as to represent your employment sector.

After spending two years on the Sussex TEC Board Maggie resigned because she was moving to Scotland, but she enjoyed her experience and is actively seeking similar board appointments near her new home.

3

WOMEN AND WORK

Women in non-traditional careers – Home-based employment – Self-employment – Women in public life – Voluntary work – Where the jobs will be in the future

WOMEN IN NON-TRADITIONAL CAREERS

Despite much talk about encouraging women into non-traditional careers, very little positive progress has been made. Higher education is freely available to women, but unless an interest has been encouraged at secondary school level the numbers of females wanting to study technical/specialist vocational subjects at college or university will remain low.

I wanted to study architecture at college but was told I would be the only female in the class. Although I wasn't actually barred from enrolling on the course, I got the impression that my presence would be an embarrassment. In the end, I opted for interior design, but have never felt completely satisfied with this. I wish I had been more assertive at the outset, but at that age I lacked the confidence to push myself in where I wasn't wanted.

Case study

Dr Josephine Anne Stein, now a Senior Research Fellow at the Programme of Policy Research in Engineering Science & Technology, had difficulty in getting access to laboratory equipment and technician time whilst at graduate school in the US. She found this was not just a personal problem; the white American male students had no difficulty, but her experience was shared by other females and foreign students – what she calls the 'vulnerable ones'. This was causing her difficulty in carrying out all the experiments she wanted to complete her thesis.

Finding herself unable to solve the problem, she eventually discussed it with her thesis advisor based in a different academic department who, though male, was very supportive of women. He felt her experience was a symptom of a greater problem relating to fundamental scientific objectives of the laboratory – though not in the area of her thesis research – and advised her to cut her losses and write her thesis up as soon as possible. Josie followed his advice and actually achieved her doctorate in less time than is usually needed, but felt somewhat cheated as she had been unable to do her research in as much depth as she would have wished.

TIP

- If you cannot demolish the barrier facing you, it may be best to make a positive decision to cut your losses. Frequently, the savings in frustration and stress outweigh the drawbacks, and unexpected advantages can often be obtained, such as Josie gaining her doctorate more quickly than she had originally expected.

Know when to give up, when something is too big – face up to it and accept that your sanity is worth more.
(Merav Dover, North East Thames Health Authority)

Barriers also exist at the recruitment and selection stage. Until employers make a positive effort to alter their recruitment and training programmes, women will continue to be reluctant to apply for jobs in non-traditional areas because of their own and others' preconceptions and their fear of rejection and discrimination.

The barriers facing women wishing to get into a non-traditional career include:

- traditional advertising methods which do nothing to actively dispel the preconceptions or fear of rejection or discrimination of potential female applicants
- physical selection criteria such as strength requirements or minimum height which debar many women
- selection tests with male-orientated questions
- long-established negative attitudes/behaviour patterns within companies, which discriminate against women
- employers who in the past have found women showing little interest in applying for such jobs or who have only been able to recruit a limited number of women, who use this as an excuse for not actively trying to recruit women now
- trade unions which are opposed to adults in apprentice roles and therefore negotiate upper age limits for apprentice applicants, which preclude women returners from starting a non-traditional career.

TIPS

If you want to take up work which is generally regarded as being non-traditional for women:

- Don't allow yourself to be put off by recruitment or selection procedures that are patently geared towards men – have a go at applying anyway. If you find yourself being asked to meet impossible criteria (such as physical ones) ask the potential employer to tell you whether that criterion is actually essential for the job itself. Once you get the job, you may be able to persuade your employer to alter their recruitment procedures so they are more woman-friendly.
- Accept from the outset that you may have to work harder than a man to prove yourself. Don't waste your time and energy feeling resentful about this – concentrate instead on learning to do the job that much better than a man, if that is what is needed to achieve your aims.
- Avoid becoming confrontational. If your male colleagues make discriminatory comments about you, explain that you are just a person who, like them, wants to do the job. Obviously, if you encounter blatant discrimination you must take firmer action, but try initially to defuse the situation before it becomes that serious.
- At all times, avoid the temptation to adopt the little-woman role when you need help – this will only reinforce their view that women are not capable of doing 'men's' work.
- Join the appropriate professional association and make time to attend its functions and play an active part. This will give you opportunities to meet other women in your profession and for your capability and enthusiasm to be seen. Help and encourage other women who are thinking of entering your profession, thus increasing the female support available to you and helping towards changing public assumptions about the careers open to women.

HOME-BASED EMPLOYMENT

Many individuals, both men and women, would actively welcome an opportunity to work as an employee from their own home or a location close to their home. Most are reasonably well-skilled or qualified but either lack the personality needed for self-employment or need a guaranteed regular income. The reasons they give include:

- the need to combine caring responsibilities with paid employment
- a desire to escape from the expense and physical stress of daily commuting
- lack of jobs within an acceptable travelling distance
- disabilities or health problems
- a need or desire to relocate to a different part of the country
- a desire for part-time work or flexible working hours which they can combine with studying for an academic, professional or vocational qualification.

The term 'home-based' working is used to describe any employment which is carried out from an employee's home. The term 'teleworking' has recently appeared in our language – there are numerous definitions, but basically teleworking comprises any work carried out remotely from an employer or client's main place of work which makes use of telecommunications systems/equipment. This description can be applied to anything from a travelling sales representative using a mobile phone, to a home-based worker using a computer, fax and telephone to receive/ transmit data.

A recent introduction to the UK is the telecottage or rural telecentre, which provides telecommunications facilities and office support to local business people on a bureau basis. Only a few telecottages provide much in the way of employment opportunities – these are ones that are run as a small business, taking work in from other companies and employing local people to carry out that work either in the telecottage or in their home.

There are many different types of jobs an employee could carry out remotely from their employer's premises, but an equal number would not be suitable. Typical remote working jobs could include: research, technical authorship, word processing or data input, project planning and management, book-keeping, training course design, small-scale manufacture, production or craft work, etc. Jobs which are not suitable include those which require a high degree of daily personal interaction with other people (including customers), supervisory work where it is necessary for the supervisor to physically oversee the work of the production team, or where regular access to correspondence, non-computerised information, production equipment, etc. is needed.

The arguments used to employers in favour of home-based working include:

- increased productivity (employees are less tired because they have no daily commuting; their morale is higher because they find their working conditions more congenial; less production time is lost through interruptions, distractions, sick leave, etc.)
- savings in central office overhead costs
- savings in recruitment and training costs through the retention of staff (such as those with children) who would otherwise have had to give up work   •
- access to a wider employee base (such as carers, those living in rural communities, disabled people, etc.)
- a better public image: companies are seen to be both more environmentally friendly because of the savings in energy consumption, and more caring about the community as a whole.

On the face of it, individual employees would seem to be able to benefit enormously from home-based working. However, this is only possible if the scheme is properly planned and introduced. Without this, home-based employees face a number of problems, including:

- isolation from other employees, cutting them off from the company grapevine and making it difficult for them to develop relationships with other employees
- career development problems arising from isolation and because jobs at a more senior level may not be considered suitable for home-based workers
- family problems arising from the overlap of both workspace and working time within the home
- suspicion from colleagues/bosses that the home-based worker might be spending more time drinking coffee or doing the gardening than actually working
- increased stereotyping of women as low-grade/low ambition workers.

Very few jobs for home-based workers are advertised. Apart from the small number of organizations which have introduced formal home-working schemes for existing employees, the majority of home-based employees are those who have made *ad hoc* arrangements with their employer, often for a limited period such as whilst bringing up small children or during school holidays.

See also Chapter 6.

SELF-EMPLOYMENT

Self-employment for women is on the increase. Although three times as many men than women are self-employed, the growth in self-employment over the last decade has been higher for women than men. Older people (both male and female) are more likely to be self-employed than younger people, with half being found in the 25–44 age group. Ethnic origin also has a bearing on self-employment, with Asians being more likely, and Black/Afro-Carribean races being less likely, to be found running their own business than are Whites.

There is no typical profile for the self-employed female, but studies of self-employment generally show that people tend to set up business in a field in which they have previous experience or knowledge, may well have a self-employed spouse or have had self-employed parents, employ few or no staff and often work from their home. Reasons given for women starting in self-employment include:

- a requirement for a flexible working lifestyle which can be adjusted to fit in with family commitments
- frustration at being unable as an employee to progress beyond the glass ceiling
- disillusionment with company politics and a desire to be one's own boss
- a desire to get away from the problems and expense of daily commuting

- redundancy
- a desire for mental stimulation whilst bringing up a young family
- lack of opportunities for returning to work after a career break
- a desire to move to an area (such as a rural one) where opportunities for employment are limited.

Self-employment is one area where active assistance is provided for women. Many Local Enterprise Agencies run a Women's Enterprise Centre and more of these are planned around the country. TECs often provide funding for Women Into Business courses, as do some local authorities, inner city task forces and regional rural development commissions. A typical course will cover all the business skills required and will also include assertiveness and self-confidence training and personal counselling. Many provide help with travelling and childcare costs, ongoing support after the course and access to additional training on specialist topics.

Women are well-suited to running their own business, as most of us are very good at handling a wide diversity of tasks at the same time. However, although running your own business will give you new skills, new contacts and a tremendous sense of achievement, it is very hard work and unlikely to generate much income for you in the early years.

Is self-employment right for you?

To be successful, you need to:

- be self-reliant, self-motivated and an excellent time manager
- be willing and able to make decisions and take risks
- be able to handle a wide diversity of tasks, from strategic planning, financial management, production, marketing/selling and staff management down to doing your own filing and making your own tea/ coffee
- have in-depth knowledge of your product or service as well as excellent all-round business management skills
- have excellent interpersonal and communication skills
- be able to spot and make the most of every business opportunity which arises, as soon as it arises
- be able to cope with the isolation
- manage with little or no personal income until your business begins to make a reasonable profit.

There are few barriers to self-employment for women that men don't also face. The main challenge for women is one of establishing credibility – convincing financiers, suppliers and customers that you are serious and have the ability. Many women report difficulties in raising start-up or expansion finance, stating that although bankers say they consider each loan application purely on its business merits, many view women as lacking the experience and ruthlessness required to run a successful business.

My advice, based on my own experience of running a business and also from running business start training courses and counselling small business owners/managers, is that self-employment can be extremely satisfying and is an excellent way of gaining confidence and new skills and achievements, and I firmly believe that many women are far better suited to running a small business than are many men. However, it takes a lot of hard work and determination, has a high-risk factor, and is not for those who require a guaranteed regular income or who need the daily support and camaraderie of colleagues.

TIPS

If you would like to know more about self-employment:

● Contact your local TEC and request information on their business start scheme (address available from your local Employment Service jobcentre).
● Contact your local Enterprise Agency (addresses are available from local jobcentres or from Business In The Community).
● Ask your local jobcentre and college for information about self-employment training for women.

WOMEN IN PUBLIC LIFE

Public appointments provide an ideal opportunity for starting to move into the decision-making process. The skills used in bringing up families are precisely those needed in decision-making – teamwork, negotiation, self-motivation – yet we pay people to go on courses to learn these skills when women have already learnt them.

(Baroness Jean Denton)

Most public appointments are unpaid although you may be able to claim some expenses. They can also take up a fair bit of your spare time. However, becoming active in public life is an excellent way of refining your skills, learning new ones and making influential contacts. If your paid employment provides little opportunity for you to attend or run meetings, practise your presentation or negotiating skills, keep abreast of current affairs in other fields or meet people from other walks of life, why not consider offering your services in public life?

Opportunities for positions include:

– standing for election as a local councillor
– local health authority board member
– school governor
– committee member of a voluntary organization or charity
– committee member of a professional trade association, local Chamber of Commerce or women's network
– trade union or staff association representative

– advisory member of a government committee covering fields such as health and social services, education, the arts, environmental matters, transport, race relations, sex discrimination and consumer affairs
– non-executive director in the public, private and voluntary sectors (such positions are usually by invitation only).

Applications for the more formal public appointments are handled by the Public Appointments Unit of the Cabinet Office, who consider applications from anybody, though you need to provide the names of two appropriate sponsors. The qualities they look for include:

– able to contribute effectively in group discussions
– able to analyse problems and assess evidence impartially
– expert knowledge and experience of a particular subject (not a necessity for every appointment).

An initiative which should help increase the number of female non-executive directors is Prowess, run by Jo Cutmore of Jamieson Scott. Prowess's principal objective is: 'To improve organizational performance through the introduction of a wider diversity of views in the boardroom, initially through the appointment of top quality female and ethnic minority representatives to non-executive directorship or similar part-time posts in both public and private sector.'

It consists of a register of women with the potential to become non-executive directors and the provision of support services to them by way of a training and development programme. Funded by public and private sponsorship, Prowess aims to make under-represented groups aware that they are needed on boards, provide them with opportunities for adding to their skills and achievements, provide access to role models and information about positions that become available, and change the attitudes of both company directors and individuals in order to get more under-represented groups appointed to boards.

Entry to the register is free for the individual and can be gained either by individual application or through nomination by employers.

To gain appointment to a more informal body it is usually only necessary to show an interest and offer your services – voluntary organizations, charities and women's networks are always only too pleased to hear from volunteers.

VOLUNTARY WORK

This country would grind to a standstill if it was not for the large number of voluntary organizations with people willing to give their services for free.

Women working part time, bringing up children or temporarily between jobs are in an ideal position to become involved in the running of a voluntary organization. Even if you work full-time, you may still be able

---

TIPS: Public appointments

- Volunteering for a public appointment could benefit you if you need an opportunity to:

  - practise and improve your decision-making, negotiating, presentation or committee skills
  - gain knowledge of a wider range of fields
  - increase your circle of influential contacts
  - add to your list of achievements.

- Before committing yourself, make sure you can spare the necessary time and energy (your employer may allow you to undertake some public responsibilities as part of your job, if it is an area of direct interest to your company or would constitute good staff development).

- If you lack the initial confidence to offer your services, find a friend with whom to make a joint approach.

---

to spare a few hours a month. Voluntary organizations range from national charities to local pressure groups, but all provide similar opportunities for keeping your management skills up to date or learning new ones, and for gaining new contacts and knowledge. Until recently, potential employers have taken little notice of voluntary work, but it is now possible to use this experience to obtain vocational qualifications through the National Vocational Qualifications/Accreditation of Prior Learning (NVQ/APL) system.

Most smaller voluntary organizations are run on a shoestring and lack workers with sophisticated management skills. Many have until recently 'muddled along' on a day-to-day basis, but recent changes to the Charities Act require them to take a far more professional approach to their business activities – thus they need volunteers who can help them improve their management practices. A list of the major voluntary organizations can be obtained from the National Council for Voluntary Organizations (NCVO); alternatively, your public library or local authority will hold addresses for local organizations.

TIP

- Undertaking voluntary work can help you improve your career prospects by providing you with an opportunity to:

  - keep your existing skills up to date
  - acquire new skills
  - add to your list of achievements
  - gain vocational qualifications
  - develop your knowledge of alternative career fields
  - increase your circle of contacts
  - get you back into the habit of working after a career break or long spell of unemployment.

Most voluntary positions are unpaid although you may get your expenses reimbursed. Under current social security rules, you can undertake voluntary work (including paid work) for a certain amount of time each week without affecting your entitlement to unemployment benefit. For many women, working on a voluntary basis leads directly to the offer of paid employment, either with the organization with which they have been working or from contacts gained. For others, it opens up an interest in a new career field which they had not previously considered.

WHERE THE JOBS WILL BE IN THE FUTURE

Most of the 1.4 million growth in the labour force since 1984 is accounted for by women, and although the rate of growth is expected to be much slower over the next decade than it was in the 1980s, this trend is expected to continue, with the prediction that the majority of the growth (80 per cent to the year 2006) will be accounted for by women. The growth will occur predominantly in the older age group, with those workers aged over 35 increasing by almost 3 million between 1993 and 2006, whereas the number of workers in the 20–34 age group is projected to fall by 1.5 million over the same period. (Statistics obtained from the Labour Market Quarterly Report, Employment Department, May 1993).

The main implication is that there will be fewer young people available for employment and employers will need to modify their traditional pattern of recruiting mainly young new entrants to the labour market. They will instead have to consider alternative recruitment sources such as women, older people, ethnic minorities and disabled people.

Most employers found few recruitment problems during the recent recession but longer-term skill shortage problems have not been solved. Problems in meeting demands for key skills will arise from both the reduction of young entrants to the labour market and increased competition.

The 1980s and early 1990s have seen a substantial change to the type of jobs which employers need to fill. Primary and manufacturing sectors have lost 0.75 million jobs, compared to gains of 1.3 million jobs in business and miscellaneous service sectors and 2.1 million in higher level occupations such as managers, professionals and technicians. Part-time jobs have increased by 1 million and self-employment by 0.5 million. Requirements for managers, administrators, professionals and associated occupations are expected to grow by 25 per cent in the current decade, compared to a growth rate of just 7 per cent in the economy as a whole.

Changes in organizational structures have led to jobs requiring a wider range of qualifications and skills and greater individual flexibility. Employers will need to make the most of their existing workforce by providing them with ongoing training and skills developing/updating, and must be prepared to offer more flexible working practices and competitive wage rates in order to retain their existing workers and attract new ones, particularly as much of the shortfall of workers will need to be met by recruiting women with children.

The areas where greatest recruitment difficulties are seen are in high technology and in professional, technical and craft occupations (those occupations where long lead-times are needed to develop the required skills). The qualities that future employees will need include:

- *Abilities and attributes* like problem-solving, creativity, flexibility, business-thinking and taking responsibility;
- *Ways of thinking* such as being able to recognise a problem and set about solving it without supervision, or to spot a potential problem and avoid it;
- *Ways of working* such as playing an effective part in a team and understanding the possible consequences of a group action or decision;
- *Outlooks on work* like a desire for continuous improvement or getting things right first time.

(Crown Copyright, reproduced from Employment Department Skills and Enterprise Briefing, October 1992: 'Training for Tomorrow's Changing World', by permission of the Skills and Enterprise Network.)

The increase of the widespread introduction of information technology will continue and applications such as word processing, desktop publishing, database design/maintenance, spreadsheets, computer-aided design and computer modelling will be found in even the smallest firms.

In summary, the future looks reasonably good for women, but only if we ensure that we:

- have the right qualities and skills
- are willing to undertake training on a regular basis to update these skills and learn new ones
- keep ourselves informed about labour market trends and the type of vocations which will be most required
- constantly remind employers about how those skills traditionally seen as being typically 'female' skills meet company requirements for flexibility, teamworking, etc.
- continue to campaign for family-friendly working practices.

4

PERSONALITY, POLITICS, POWER AND THE ART OF PERSUASION

Personality – Assertiveness – Image – Effective communication – Identifying and asserting authority – Politics and power – The art of persuasion – Managing your work relationships

The words 'authority' and 'influence' have a nice ring to them; 'politics' and 'power' create visions of manipulation and self-aggrandisement. Women are renowned for modesty and self-effacement but these have no place on the rungs of the career ladder; without power, we cannot establish and assert our authority.

> Women are on the 'horns of a dilemma' when it comes to assertiveness, power-seeking behaviour. If a female manager does not display the kind of behaviour that is traditionally associated with successful management, then the male managers will feel she is not a very effective manager. On the other hand, if she does, many male and female colleagues will see her . . . as 'hostile, maladjusted and overcontrolling', that is 'too often "leadership" qualities for a man are judged as traits of hostility and aggression in a woman'. Nevertheless, research indicates that women managers who adopt modes of assertive behaviour report increased confidence and effectiveness.
>
> (Davidson and Cooper, 1992, p. 62)

To progress through the glass ceiling, it is not enough just to manage yourself and your work effectively. However tempting it is to put your head down, get on with the job and avoid getting involved in office politics, you must also establish good relationships and influence with the people who matter – this depends on:

- knowing the extent of your authority
- knowing where the power lies in your company and how you can use it to your advantage
- making the most of your personality and projecting the right image
- communicating effectively
- establishing rapport with others.

Without this, you will miss opportunities for exchanging ideas and views with others, broadening your knowledge and understanding, and gaining their co-operation in shared tasks and general support for you as a person. You will also have difficulty in getting your skills, qualities and achievements widely recognised.

PERSONALITY

Our personality is created by our innate character, influenced by both our background and experience and by our own desires. We may be unable to change the basic nature of our personality, but we can learn to understand it and make it work for us. For instance, we may by nature be a quiet, self-effacing person but assertiveness training can teach us how to project a confident and competent image. We may never feel fully comfortable but we can, with practice, become able to stand up for ourselves when it really matters.

Personality shows itself in two ways – firstly through the style or manner in which we approach and deal with situations and people, and secondly through our temperament, the way we react and respond, i.e. how we feel or are affected by the things that happen to us. The way you approach life and react to it is very important – if others see you as reticent and self-effacing, bombastic, or temperamental and changeable, you will not be thought suitable for a position requiring a calm, collected, authoritative and tactful character.

There are many forms of personality test available for a fee of around £25 upwards. Details can be obtained from most professional career analysts; if your own personnel department uses personality tests in recruitment, ask to take one as part of your career development plan.

> When I was invited to take the Myers-Briggs Type Indicator test as part of a Women In Management course, I was very cynical about it, but to my surprise I found the results almost exactly matched the way I felt about myself. Analysing the results under the guidance of the counsellor helped me understand where my strengths lie and become aware of where I needed to make an effort to change and improve. I have since taken a different style of personality test and found that that too gave valid results.

To some extent, psychometric tests reflect the way you feel about yourself at the time of taking the test. If you are feeling low and depressed, the result will be subtly different to the result you would get if you took the same test after just having gained a major achievement, when you felt good about yourself. It is important to ensure that you consider the results of all such tests within the context of your circumstances at that time. When taking a psychometric test, ensure the tester is properly qualified to administer the test and counsel you afterwards. The British Psychological Society (see address in Further Information section) publishes a Directory of Chartered Occupational Psychologists and maintains a Register of Occupational Testers.

Are you a square peg in a round hole?

Beware of getting stuck in a job for which you have the wrong personality – you will never feel completely comfortable and will achieve less than someone of the right type. In the worst case, you will end up feeling a failure, destroying your self-confidence and setting your career back many years.

You can carry out your own form of personality test by working through the questionnaire in the Appendix and then comparing your characteristics against your assessment of a colleague in a job at the level you are aiming for or with an advertisement for a job which you think you would like, then thinking carefully about whether you have the right personality for that type of job. If you feel you are intrinsically the right type of person but need to ensure that those in authority will recognise you as having those qualities, list up the improvements you need to make and work on them one at a time, or seek professional training.

ASSERTIVENESS

Assertiveness is the art of getting your own needs and wants met without preventing others from getting theirs (achieving a win/win outcome). It is not to be confused with aggressiveness (getting your own way through trampling all over other people – win/lose) or non-assertiveness/passiveness (allowing others to get their way at your expense – lose/win). The way you behave to others is expressed not only by the words you use but also by the tone and level of your voice and your body language.

None of us are totally aggressive, assertive or non-assertive by nature – our behaviour at any given time depends on the situation, our relationship with the people we are dealing with, their attitudes and personality, and the way that we feel about ourselves at that point in time. It is not uncommon for the behaviour of individuals – both men and women – to swing from one extreme (aggressive) to the other (non-assertive) in different situations, or sometimes even in the same situation. However, we are all capable of learning to become more assertive in all situations, and in learning to handle aggressive or passive people – though practice is needed to perfect our skills.

Because many people believe women incapable of assertiveness, our behaviour is frequently labelled as being one extreme or the other because that is what is expected from us, whereas in a man similar behaviour is considered assertive. By believing that we can be assertive and working on improving our own behaviour, this stereotyping will eventually cease as the results we achieve influence the thinking of those around us.

It is easy enough to be assertive when we are in a situation where we feel fully confident and comfortable. Assertive behaviour becomes more difficult when:

– facing unfamiliar or difficult people

- the subject matter or general situation is unfamiliar to us
- trying to negotiate with people not willing to negotiate or whose wants clash with ours
- having to reprimand or complain to others
- being denied what we consider to be our rights; being treated unfairly
- we do not feel fully confident about achieving our required outcome.

In fact, in any situation were we feel less than 100 per cent confident about ourselves, our ability or the situation in general, or where we are facing conflict.

Why be assertive?

As well as not getting the outcome you require, behaving anything other than assertively causes stress, which will affect you adversely both physically and mentally, both in the immediate situation and in the future. As well as feeling bad yourself about your behaviour, you will affect the way others think of you and therefore the way they treat you, and it will be harder for you in the future to regain your assertiveness.

The effects of aggression

Many people use aggression as either a means of intimidating others or as a cover for their own lack of confidence. When faced with an aggressive person we either react aggressively ourselves, or feel intimidated and become passive, letting the other person get their own way. If we instigate the aggression, the other person will either react with aggression, or will become passive but feel resentful about our behaviour.

TIPS

- Increase your awareness of assertiveness by analysing your own and others' behaviour in specific situations, and by taking professional training.
- Familiarise yourself with the body language signals that signify the different types of behaviour – learn how to display the right signals yourself and interpret the signals others give out.
- Remind yourself of your needs and rights, of the needs and rights of others, and of the advantages of acting assertively. Prepare as fully as possible beforehand, and picture yourself achieving your desired outcome so that you increase your self-confidence.
- If you feel yourself becoming aggressive towards others, remind yourself of both the harm it will do and the other person's right to be treated fairly.
- If you feel yourself becoming intimidated, remind yourself of your own rights and needs, and also of the harm that acting non-assertively will do you.
- Aim to treat others at all times in the way you yourself would like to be treated, regardless of the way they are treating you.
- Challenge (assertively!) all comments about women not being able to act assertively.

The normal male reaction is to face aggression with aggression – if we become aggressive with a man we are likely to have a fight on our hands; if we become non-assertive, we hand all the power over to them. Either way, we are unlikely to achieve the result we desire.

IMAGE

Image is important for women generally – whoever you are, you need the power to project the image *you* want, to stand up and make people notice you rather than just waiting to be noticed. Image includes our clothes, our hair, how we sit and stand, how we respond to others. It is within all of us to change our image. Often, people want to make me powerless, they don't want to listen to what I have to say – I decide to put out an image of power, to say 'yes, I *am* here, and will still be here tomorrow'.

The image we project is important both for our own self-esteem and because it influences the way others view us.

First impressions

You never get a second chance to make a first impression.

We all make snap judgements when meeting someone for the first time, categorising them on our past experiences of people with similar characteristics. First impressions may often be wrong but because it is human nature to dislike admitting having made a mistake, it can be very difficult to get others to change their first impression of us. It is therefore very important that we make a good first impression every time we meet someone new.

Self-image

We have the power to decide on the image we wish to project but it is difficult to make ourselves appear to be something which clashes with our inner view of ourself (self-image). We need to:

– decide on the image we want to project
– identify the type of behaviour, body language and dress needed to project that image
– consider how our basic personality equates with that image
– adapt the image so it sits comfortably with our personality
– practise projecting our chosen image at every opportunity.

Dress

Dress for success.

Dress plays a very important part in both the way we feel about ourselves and the image we project.

I fought for years against the concept of 'power dressing' but finally had to accept that I would not be viewed as a competent, professional businesswoman unless I dressed in the generally accepted fashion. I have now found that knowing that the first impression of me that people get fits my desired image has done wonders for my confidence.

TIPS

- Look at the type of clothes the people at the level you want to get to are wearing, and dress for that level, not your current level – continuously projecting the image of a higher-level person encourages others to realise you have the capabilities for that level.
- Ensure the style you choose suits you. Avoid wearing tailored suits with short skirts if you are not happy with the shape of your legs – instead, stick to longer-length skirts and co-ordinated jackets – it may not be high fashion but you will feel much better about yourself.
- Ensure you feel comfortable, both physically and mentally. If your waistline has expanded, don't force yourself into too-tight clothes. If you feel awkward showing your knees and thighs, avoid short skirts when you know you will be sitting down with your legs on view.
- If you get caught out wearing inappropriate clothes, draw attention to them by saying something like 'it's amazing how much more innovative I feel when wearing casual clothes' – by doing this you will be able to feel good about the situation instead of feeling awkward.

Practical exercise: What impression do you make on others?

(1)   Do you enjoy and look forward to meeting new people?

(2)   Do you always prepare in advance for the meeting, planning your image and attitude and dressing appropriately?

(3)   Does your attitude and image reflect the job you would like to have, rather than the job you currently have?

(4)   Do you walk into the room confidently and naturally?

(5)   Do you feel comfortable shaking hands with other people, particularly other women?

(6)   Do you look the other person in the eye and smile at them?

(7)   Do you make a specific point of noting the other person's name and face and personal information about them, so that when you next meet they will know you have taken the trouble to remember them as an individual?

(8)   Does your body language portray you as confident and knowledgeable, nervous, or aggressive?

(9)   Do you put your views forward confidently and assertively at the right time, getting a comfortable balance between talking too much and too little?

(10)   Do you wait for others to ask your opinion before saying anything at all, or monopolise the conversation, grabbing every opportunity to impress others with your skills and knowledge?

(11)   Do you make snap judgements about others, and do these judgements turn out to be right or wrong?

TIPS

- If you have difficulty in remembering names and faces, train yourself to listen properly when someone is introduced to you, instead of thinking how you are going to introduce yourself back to them. Try repeating the other person's name – 'Hello Joe, my name is Mary' – to help you to fix their name and face firmly in your mind.
- Study how other people act when meeting someone for the first time and learn from their mistakes and successes.
- Analyse how you judge people when meeting them for the first time – note which of their characteristics make the most impression on you and the standards and prior experiences by which you judge them. Is the other person likely to be judging you by similar standards and experiences?
- Put yourself in the right frame of mind before meeting new people. Each occasion is an opportunity – to gain information and knowledge, to demonstrate your abilities, to gain a new contact or friend. Positively welcome each chance to meet new people and concentrate on the opportunities open to you.

EFFECTIVE COMMUNICATION

Communication is a two-way process. You need to ensure that the other person understands what you say and that you have properly understood them – this is not always as easy to do as it sounds. Poor communication is a serious barrier to interpersonal relations; if misunderstandings arise because one or other of you is not communicating properly, you may not get the action or result you expected and this could reflect badly on you. It may also make the other person reluctant to deal with you in the future because they fear repeated problems and misunderstandings. Poor communication will seriously affect your career prospects.

The 'language' and behaviour patterns used by men and women, and by people from different ethnic cultures, can vary widely. It is important to be aware of these differences to avoid causing yourself problems by misinterpreting the other person's meaning, or by your words and actions being misinterpreted by them.

The words we use form only a small proportion of our communication. Words are important, but even more important is our non-verbal communication – the tone and volume of our voice, our expression and body language. Non-verbal communication is particularly relevant when we or the other person say something we do not really mean or feel; no matter how carefully we choose our words, our body language is likely to send out a conflicting message and either confuse the other person or make them realise that we are insincere.

The same goes for written communication. We may have a brilliant idea to convey, but if the look of our message – the paper we use, the way it is typed or written, the spelling and grammar, etc. – is of a poor standard, the reader will be unlikely to give much credence to the content.

Hearing what someone says is not the same as listening to them. Developing good listening skills is an essential part of good communication – if you do not listen properly, you may hear what you expected them to say, not what they actually said. Remember the saying 'You have two ears but only one mouth – spend twice as much time listening as talking'.

TIPS

Practice:

- Becoming more aware of your own body language and the non-verbal signals you give out.
- Interpreting and understanding the non-verbal signals others give out, in order to find out their true feelings and avoid getting into conflict with them.
- Familiarising yourself with the 'language' and behaviour patterns used by men and people from other cultural backgrounds.
- Listening properly at all times.
- Controlling the conversation by steering the other person back to the main topic in hand if they start to drift off.
- Checking you have properly heard and understood the other person, by summarising the points they made and asking them to confirm that you have correctly understood them.
- Confirming at the end of the conversation the points agreed, to ensure there is no misunderstanding.
- Ensuring all your written communication conveys the image you want to project.

A smile

A smile costs nothing, but gives much. It enriches those who receive, without making poorer those who give. It takes but a moment, but the memory of it sometimes lasts for ever. None is so rich or mighty that they can get along without it, and none is so poor but that they can be made rich by it. A smile creates happiness in the home, fosters goodwill in business and is the countersign of friendship. It brings rest to the weary, cheer to the discouraged, sunshine to the sad, and it is nature's best antidote for trouble. Yet it cannot be bought, begged, borrowed or stolen, for it is something that is of no value to anyone until it is given away. Some people are too tired to give you a smile. Give them one of yours, as none needs a smile so much as they who have no more to give.

(Anon)

IDENTIFYING AND ASSERTING AUTHORITY

Responsibility, authority and accountability go hand in hand. It is no good being given the responsibility for something if you are not also given the authority that is needed to carry out that responsibility, and are prepared to take that responsibility and be held accountable for achieving it.

Every job carries a certain level of authority and it is important that you know the extent to which you are empowered to make decisions and implement action. Job descriptions usually concentrate on describing the tasks the job involves; rarely do they lay down the precise levels of authority that go with the job.

If your job description does not fully spell out your level of authority, seek clarification. When given new work to do, ascertain your precise responsibilities and the level of your authority and clarify to whom you will be accountable for achieving the required results. By discussing this frankly with your boss and showing that you actively welcome the chance to make decisions, you will be able to negotiate a higher degree of authority than you might otherwise have been given.

Authority needs to be both given and taken. Not only do you need to be granted the authority to do something – you must also act on that authority. It is often tempting to refer decisions to others and make them responsible for any element of risk, but if you have been given the authority, you must yourself take the decisions and be responsible for the outcome.

> Take risks – trust your instinct and do what that tells you. If your instinct warns you not to take that risk, listen to it, but ask yourself why it is warning you. Could the reason that you feel afraid be because other people are telling you that you don't have the ability and you are allowing them to undermine your confidence?

> It is really important to take risks with one's life. We all want security, but nothing in life is secure – life is about constant movement, constant change – you have to be able to take risks to keep up with it.

Take care not to usurp the authority of others. Your bosses and colleagues may be more than happy to delegate some of their responsibilities to you, but if you don't first get their agreement, they may feel you are trying to take over their job. Not only will you alienate them, you may also end up having your existing level of authority reduced, to keep you from 'stepping out of line' in the future.

Ensure that all your staff are fully aware of the authority you are giving them, and then make them accountable for their actions. Gradually increasing the degree of authority you allow your staff is a good development process for them, but make it clear that you also hold them accountable for their decisions. Don't put them under too much pressure by expecting them to be perfect immediately – stand by them when they make mistakes and help them learn from these.

Women as decision-makers

Women are often portrayed as lacking the ability or confidence to make decisions. This is nonsense, but may stem from the tendency for women to adopt the 'consensus' approach, seeking to consult and discuss with their colleagues before reaching a decision. Men who adopt the dictatorial role, driving their decision through because they are the individual responsible, view women as weak and lacking authority. They overlook the problems which a dictatorship creates.

TIP

- If you are accused of being a poor decision-maker because you prefer the consultative, consensus approach, point out the improvements in co-operation and morale that this generates.

POLITICS AND POWER

Hitch your wagon to a rising star.

We need to be aware of acquiring, exercising and using power. If we don't have power ourselves, we have to borrow it from those who do have it, in order to build up a power base of support for ourselves.

Many women feel unhappy about the concept of power and company politics. We play down our achievements and often feel uncomfortable about receiving compliments, thus denying ourselves power; we dislike playing 'power games'.

My boss told me I would never get on unless I cultivated the right contacts. I said I was being paid to work, not socialise, and that using my time to develop contacts in order to gain personal advancement seemed immoral. He made me feel confused and upset – I ended up making a compromise which achieved nothing, getting behind with my work *and* failing to properly establish good relationships with the people who mattered.

Having influence and making use of it is not immoral, so long as we are aware of the effect this has on others and ensure that using our influence to gain success does not harm them. However much we may dislike it, it is a fact of life that unless we develop our influence with the people that matter, we run the risk of being overlooked in the promotion stakes.

THE ART OF PERSUASION

The ability to create and foster good interpersonal relations is the most valuable skill any manager can have. Without the co-operation of our bosses, peers and staff, we become isolated and depressed and our career prospects suffer.

TIPS: Politics and power

- Learn to spot the various cliques and 'inner circles' that exist within your company, and get to know how these groups relate to each other. Listen carefully to find out their views about company matters – the board may have issued written Values Statements and Objectives, but it is the 'inner circles' which influence company culture. Keep your ears and eyes open and your mouth shut until you are sure you have got a grip on the various levels of company politics.

- Once you know who in your company has influence, work on establishing good relations with the people that matter. You don't need to 'curry favour' – treat them as you would wish to be treated yourself. A good way to start developing a relationship is to ask them for their opinion about something ('stroking their ego') – few people can resist flattery if it is genuine.

- Position yourself, both mentally and physically, so that you can influence those with power. At meetings, sitting next to, or directly opposite, the Chair or the person with the most power helps you increase your own influence.

- Don't minimise your achievements – you have earned any credit you are given. When the opportunity arises, ensure that those in authority hear about your achievements – if you practise looking for the right opportunity you will not be viewed as bragging or bigheaded.

- Avoid criticising others at all times – it is quite possible that the person you are talking to plays golf with the person you are criticising, or that the criticism will get back to them by a roundabout route.

- Listen to company gossip – much of it will be rumour or exaggeration but there is usually some basis of fact – by listening rather than joining in the talk you can avoid being labelled a gossip yourself.

- Practise identifying the type of people who get on quickly in your company, and analyse what it is about them that makes them successful. 'Hitching your wagon' to a person expected to get on, so that you can rise with them, is useful, but beware of the possible dangers – if they fall out of favour, so might you; or you might become so closely linked with them in other people's eyes that you are never seen to be a success in your own right.

- Be aware of the effect your own success has on the people around you. Your boss may feel put out if you are singled out for special treatment by the department head – tell your boss that much of the credit for your ability lies with them because of the way they have trained and developed you (it may not be entirely true, but it will keep them happy!).

- Be prepared for your peers to feel jealous or threatened – they may respond by congratulating you to your face, then put you down behind your back. Developing good relationships with them before you become a success will help to minimise this. Concentrate on showing you still relate well to the people you trust; if possible, enlist their help in dispelling malicious rumours like 'It's obvious, she must be sleeping with him'.

- Once you have gained influence, make time every so often to review whether or not you are making as much use of it as you can and to ensure that you are not abusing it by using your power to harm others. In particular, think whether your influence enables you to help other women who might be facing the barriers that you have managed to break through – avoid becoming the sort of person who says 'I got here under my own steam – why should I help them?'

Are women better than men at interpersonal relations?

Women are widely considered to be better than men at human relationships, because of our traditional roles as homemaker, child-raiser and community worker. A woman bringing up children learns to impart knowledge, instructions and discipline and develops good negotiating skills – abilities which can be refined for use with adults. Our superior ability to form good relationships (or the perception of our superiority) may be why more women than men specialise in fields such as teaching, human resources and equal opportunities.

These skills may to some extent be naturally inbred in women, but many of us find relationships at work a major reason for both stress and lack of advancement. Davidson and Cooper (1992, p. 98) in a questionnaire survey found that women cited the following problems:

(1)   Members of opposite sex seem uncomfortable working with women because of their sex.
(2)   Experiencing prejudiced attitudes at work because of their sex from members of the same sex and opposite sex.
(3)   Feeling uncomfortable on training courses when a member of the minority sex.
(4)   Sexual harassment.
(5)   Lack of encouragement from superiors.
(6)   Lack of support from people at work.

It is therefore not unusual for women to have problems with their working relationships. If you find you are having problems, don't worry that there is something wrong with you – instead, concentrate on learning how to improve your skills. You may feel you have to make more of an effort in this area than a man would – instead of wasting your time feeling resentful, concentrate on all the positive advantages you stand to gain. Wherever possible (without being aggressive) remind people about the superior interpersonal skills that women (are perceived to) have, and bear in mind that it may be the other person, not you, who has the problem.

Negotiating and persuading

Roget's Thesaurus links the following words, among others, with 'persuasion': authority, charisma, convince, flatter, impress, influence, inspire, motivate, patronage, power, request. The ability to successfully persuade others depends to a great extent on both our personality and our presentation and negotiating skills. Like all skills, these can be learned and improved upon.

A successful negotiator is someone who can obtain an agreement whereby all parties have their needs satisfied, have a desire to fulfil their commitments and are willing to enter into future negotiations.

A successful presenter is someone who not only puts facts and viewpoints over to others clearly and without misunderstandings, but who also makes an impact, arouses interest and inspires their audience to respond to them.

Many women feel unhappy about negotiating and presenting for a variety of reasons including:

- lack of assertiveness and self-confidence
- fear of failure
- being unsure as to what outcome they want to achieve
- being unsure about the extent of their power
- failing to prepare properly
- not wishing to get into conflict
- failing to identify the correct person with whom to negotiate
- lack of opportunity to practise and improve their skills
- others' belief that women are poor negotiators or presenters.

Case study

Dr. Annette Lawson of ETHOS, when working as head of department at a British university, had been promised by the dean of her faculty that she could have a year's sabbatical leave of absence to go to the US if she should receive invitations to work as a visiting scholar. On receiving a number of prestigious invitations, Annette formally asked the dean to forward her request to the vice chancellor, only to be told by the dean that he could not deal with this as he was himself about to go off on tour. He was, in any event, about to leave the university for more prestigious pastures. On trying to find alternative support, Annette found she had fallen into a 'political vacuum' – a new dean had been appointed and a new professor would be taking on her own and another department which were to merge.

I found my negotiations with these people completely demeaning, humiliating and destructive – it was obvious they would not honour any commitment promised by the departing dean, and I found the power politics impossible to understand and manage. Eventually, I was invited to a discussion where I found myself facing two men – the vice chancellor and secretary general – I had not been told that I would be seeing two people and had not thought to take anyone along with me for support. Although they said the faculty could not afford to be without me, they also told me I was 'too good for my own university and would be much better off at Stanford or Berkeley'. I ended up feeling completely undervalued. When I asked one man what he would do in my place, I was told 'I would never *be* in your place'. When I sought support from my colleagues (all male), my 'bosses' accused me of gossiping. Despite close friendships with many of my colleagues, none would actually put pen to paper in my support.

On looking back, Annette feels that the barrier she faced occurred mainly because she was at a structural disadvantage – she held a senior position with all the authority of head of department but was deemed low in the academic hierarchy because, due to having taken a career break, she had not been promoted above lecturer level. Men of her age and ability but without her career break were now occupying positions as professors. This left her having to negotiate from a position in which no man would have found himself.

Reflecting on her experience, Annette believes it is vital that we have sufficient conviction in our personal value so we can negotiate from a position of inner strength instead of feeling that we are weak and leaving ourselves even more vulnerable than we otherwise would be in conditions of continuing structural disadvantage. Other women, especially in organised groups, can be a good source of support.

Practical exercise: Are you a good negotiator?

(1)   Do you always prepare fully beforehand?
(2)   Do you consider negotiating an enjoyable game or something to be avoided where possible?
(3)   Do you consider negotiating to be competitive or co-operative?
(4)   How uncomfortable do you feel when facing direct conflict?
(5)   Do you aim for an outcome which satisfies you, or which satisfies all the parties involved?
(6)   How comfortable do you feel when negotiating something which affects you personally?
(7)   Do you find out beforehand the extent and limits of the other person's power and authority?
(8)   How comfortable do you feel when negotiating with someone of a higher status?
(9)   How well do you think when under pressure?
(10) Do you make good use of probing questions?
(11) Are you reticent about your own requirements and opinions, or do you say more than you ought?
(12) Do you make good use of silences or always rush to fill them?
(13) Do you decide beforehand the concessions you are willing to make to the other person?
(14) Do you let yourself get emotionally involved?

Effective presentation

Your audience may be an individual, a small group or hundreds of people, but the same basic rules apply as for negotiating: PREPARE, PRACTISE, PRESENT.

TIPS: Negotiating and persuading

- Preparation:

    - find out as much as you can about your audience: their needs, interests, the extent of their authority, questions they are likely to ask, concessions they may be prepared to give, how committed they are likely to be to reaching an agreement
    - collect all the information you will need to answer questions
    - clarify your own objectives: identify your preferred outcome; think about possible creative alternative outcomes which will satisfy both sides
    - clarify your own power: you know more than the other person about what it is you want to achieve; you have the power to turn down any deal which does not meet your needs; if backed into a corner, you have the power to request time to consider the options open to you or to collect more information
    - look for others on whom you can call for support, if needed, and ensure they are fully briefed
    - put yourself in the right frame of mind: picture yourself getting the outcome you want; try to disassociate yourself as an individual from the negotiations (the more emotionally involved you get and the more important the outcome to you, the weaker your negotiating position will be). Ask yourself whether it will really be the end of the world if you don't get a satisfactory outcome
    - decide on the image you are going to project.

- Practise:

    - writing down all the likely areas of discussion and your dialogue, then practise out loud in front of a mirror or someone you trust
    - negotiating minor deals with other people before going into the 'big one'.

- Presentation:

    - get the other person to come to you or pick a neutral venue so that you are not operating on their turf
    - pick an appropriate time: negotiations proceed better during or after a meal; ensure that neither of you is going to have to rush off somewhere else before you have finished
    - take time to 'arrive', to assess your surroundings, the other person – take a deep breath and then breathe out, relax your shoulders and neck muscles, make eye contact and smile
    - sit side by side or across the corner of the table rather than directly facing one another
    - don't rush straight into your dialogue – take as long as it needs to build up rapport with the other person. 'Stroke' their ego by asking them about themselves, their job, etc.
    - make good use of your personality: allow your warmth and enthusiasm to inspire the other person
    - use probing questions to find out all the facts; echo these back to the other person in your own words to ensure you have correctly understood them – stress that you are looking for an outcome which suits *both* of you; that you want to work with them, not against them. Stress

the advantages they will gain; use phrases such as 'working in part-nership' and 'helping each other'
- don't rush to give concessions or suggest alternative solutions – wait until the other person asks for this or you can see you are heading towards a stalemate
- spend more time listening than talking; don't rush to fill up any silences
- be aware of body language – both yours and theirs
- co-operate on minor points to gain their co-operation with the major ones
- learn to spot when the other person is ready to reach agreement; beware of talking yourself out of the agreement once you have reached that stage
- sum up the agreements reached and ensure you both understand the actions you need to take and by when.

- Remember that:

  - you get what you expect: go in with high aspirations and the belief in them and your rights and ability to obtain them
  - negotiating is a game: like all games, the more you practise, the better you will become.

TIPS: Presenting

- 'Presence' is the ability to give your complete attention to your audience; to be fully aware and in touch with what is happening at each moment and the impact you are having. If your audience begins to lose attention, ask them an interesting question or call a short break.
- Facts alone do not hold an audience's attention for long. Inspire and enthuse them by making them feel emotionally involved: ask yourself 'Why do *I* care about this?' 'Why should *they* care?'. Let your passion for your subject come through.
- Let your personality come across; make your audience fully aware of you and want to listen to what you have to say.
- When speaking to a number of people, talk to one as an individual for a few moments, then do the same with another person, so that they each feel personally involved.
- Talk slightly slower than you would in normal conversation, and make sure your voice can be heard. Remember to smile; use your hands to demonstrate your enthusiasm but watch out for irritating habits such as playing with your pen, which will distract the audience's attention from what you are saying.

MANAGING YOUR WORK RELATIONSHIPS

Being the boss

Some subordinates, often both men and women in the older age groups, feel uncomfortable about working for a female boss, particularly if that boss is younger than them. Typical assumptions are that women bosses:

- nag
- are bossy
- don't like making decisions
- won't delegate
- lack confidence
- lack authority
- can't negotiate successfully
- can't assert themselves
- collapse under pressure
- think more about their family than their job.

Women, particularly when being promoted from sub-management level, often have difficulty in deciding where their loyalties lie. We are reluctant to lose the camaraderie of our former peers and concentrate on being liked rather than on establishing our new authority. This may feel more comfortable, but what happens when you have to discipline one of your staff? Also, do your peers and boss regard you as a proper manager, or do they still think of you as one of the support team?

Female leadership styles often differ to those preferred by men, giving rise to male assumptions that women do not make good leaders. There is no single right way to manage staff – we have to find the style that suits our personality, the people we manage, the type of work we do and which gets the best results.

Competence comes from experience and confidence – don't be afraid to try out several leadership styles until you find the most effective one. Your aim should be to create a skilled, loyal team on which you know you can rely and who are willing to make that extra bit of effort for you. Give them interesting and challenging work, be fair but firm, and remember to praise them, not just for some special performance but also for their regular work. Train them up so that the more capable ones are able to do your level of work – the more you can delegate to them without affecting the overall productivity of the team, the more time you will have to expand your own skills and contacts.

TIPS

- Be clear in your own mind what you want your status to be. Aim to become a full member of your boss's team and be seen as such – your staff will form their own team which you can lead, but you need to build up your image as a more senior person who is capable of standing in for the boss in their absence.
- Make time to establish good relationships with your peers and your boss, including other women at your level and above in your own or another department or company, to gain companionship and support.
- Don't allow men to criticise your leadership style just because this differs from theirs. Bring the good results you get to their attention, to illustrate that a different style can be just as effective.

Building rapport with your peers

With companies moving increasingly to a 'flat' hierarchy, the need to inter-act with colleagues from both your own and other departments or com-panies increases. You can create career opportunities through establishing good relationships with your peers, particularly those outside your own group who may be able to highlight your skills to their bosses or tell you about forthcoming vacancies. Where you and your colleagues are involved in team activities, the achievements of the team will be directly related to how well – or how badly – you all work together.

TIPS

- Sometimes women feel they need to act like a man in order to be accepted by male colleagues. You shouldn't need to do this but you may have to make some concessions – such as making the time to occasionally join them for a drink after work (make sure you buy a round or you risk being considered, and treated as, someone different to them, which will not help you integrate). You will have to decide for yourself whether the benefits to be gained from such concessions outweigh the drawbacks.
- A typical situation often arises at meetings, where the woman is auto-matically expected to be the one to serve the coffee or clear the cups away afterwards. I get round this by asking whoever is nearest the coffee pot to pour it and by either leaving the dirty cups, making a joke about men being better at washing up than I am, or suggesting a rota system. Although I hate leaving a room in a mess, I find it better to suppress my natural inclination to tidy up, in order to avoid building an 'inappropriate' role for myself.
- If it is within your power, invite another woman onto the team to help balance things up and get the men more used to working with women, but take care not to be seen as 'ganging up' on them.
- Take the time to get to know each of the men as individuals. Once they each realise you are not trying to get the better of them, you will find it easier to gain their co-operation.
- Avoid proving how good you are by criticising others or stressing mistakes they have made. It is one thing to let people know about your skills and successes; comparing others to yourself, to their detriment, will not endear you to either the person you are criticising or to others who hear you – the onlookers will wonder whether they will be your next target. If you need to tell someone about a mistake they have made because this has caused you problems, speak to them in private.
- Women often report having their suggestions at meetings ignored, only to find that five minutes later the same suggestion is put forward by a man and listened to. If you find this happening, review your own behaviour – is it assertive enough? Are you speaking too quietly? Sit close enough to the Chair to be heard, and ask them to go back to the point you made, e.g. 'We didn't actually discuss my suggestion – we need to do so before we move onto the next point'.
- Don't allow yourself to be overlooked at meetings. Men invariably speak up in order to be noticed, even if they have nothing of real importance to say. If you fail to take an active part, your male colleagues are likely to assume that you are unable or unwilling to contribute.

Some men have difficulty in treating their women colleagues as equals, perceiving them as a threat, particularly if they feel the company operates an unwritten policy of promoting the 'token woman' to positions of authority. Often, the threat to women comes from incompetent, rather than competent, male colleagues who are scared of being shown up by a woman. The situation is exacerbated when you are more highly qualified than your male peers – either because you felt the need for qualifications to prove your competence or because you are more experienced and capable but have not yet gained the promotion you merit.

Getting on with your boss

Your boss has power – to either give you the chance to develop and grow, or to hold you back. Few of us have the luxury of being able to choose our boss – we have to learn to make the best of what we get.

All relationships are based on understanding, good communication, mutual respect and trust and, not least, 'chemistry'. The best working relationships are often formed with people whose thought processes and values are the same as ours. This is one reason why men choose men to work with them – subconsciously they look for someone with whom they 'click' – who shares their interests and outlook. While the majority of senior and middle managers continue to be male, how can we overcome such subconscious discrimination?

TIPS

- To establish rapport between different personality types, both sides must recognise the need and be willing to work at it. You can take the lead by being genuinely interested in the other person as a human being, making the time to get to know their likes, dislikes, values, language and interests. Beware of the dangers of appearing false – your interest in them must be genuine and be accurately reflected by your body language. However different your personalities are, it is always possible to find some common ground.

- If you are interviewed by someone with whom you find difficulty in establishing rapport, ask yourself how closely you will need to work with them and whether the possible personality problems are likely to affect your work and prospects. If you feel you will have difficulty in overcoming the problem, seriously consider looking for an alternative job opportunity.

- If you find yourself in an untenable personality clash with your boss, concentrate on the positive aspects – such as the opportunities open to you from moving to a different job – rather than thinking of yourself as a failure. Provided you have done your best to make the relationship work, you are not to blame and have no need to feel guilty, but you must accept that your boss has more power than you and however much you feel that you are more in the right than your boss, you are likely to have to be the one to move in order to protect your career prospects.

The degree to which differences in personalities matter depends on how closely you need to work with your boss. The more senior you are, the more likely you will be to work without close supervision and there may be less need to cultivate a close relationship. However, to reach such a position you will need the support and backing of your current superior and you will only get this by gaining their trust and respect.

Do male bosses treat their female staff differently to their male staff?

As with all relationships, there is no hard and fast rule. Many women perceive themselves as being treated differently – we may feel we need to be super-efficient in order to be taken seriously; alternatively, we may use our gender in subtle (or sometimes blatant) ways to integrate ourselves with our boss.

TIPS

- Good relationships, with whichever sex, come from mutual respect and understanding – once you understand the other person's personality type it becomes easier to develop a good relationship with them, but it is up to you to recognise the need and work on building the rapport.
- Does it really matter whether your boss treats you the same as your male colleagues, provided you are given an equal level of opportunity and respect and achieve as good a level of results as them? If we are over-sensitive to this issue, perceiving inequality where it does not actually exist, we create more problems for ourselves and our female colleagues. However, if you experience different treatment which leads to discrimination against you, you must of course take action.

Working for a female boss

A female boss may provide you with a useful role model or act as your mentor. Alternatively, she may view you as a threat or be unwilling to help you because she made it on her own.

As with a male boss, you need to spend time and effort getting to know and understand her and building up a good relationship. Don't automatically expect to become bosom pals merely because you are both female, and take care not to act in a threatening manner by, for example, stressing your own more superior qualifications. If you do become good friends, be aware of how others, such as your male peers, will react. Treat your female boss as you yourself would like to be treated by a female subordinate.

Why should women have to make all the effort?

Many of us resent having to make more of an effort than a man. Actually, men do also have to make an effort, but because they go about it in a different way and tend not to talk about it between themselves or with us, it appears that they are not having to try.

The important thing to concentrate on is the benefits you will get from establishing good relationships with the people around you. It is not a battle of the sexes – your objective is to improve your personal prospects by integrating with the people with whom you work. By all means discuss with your friends any problems you encounter if this helps, but try to avoid feeling that you are in a 'them and us' situation – we will only make things worse by continuously stressing the differences between men and women where these differences can make women appear less able than men.

5

THE ROLES WOMEN PLAY

Role conflict – The token woman – Being a role model – Inappropriate roles – The feminist – Should women act like men? – Choosing your role – Mentoring – Networking

Being a feminist is about growing as individuals and having choices, and helping other women to grow as individuals.

(Joanna Foster)

There are many different roles a female manager might find herself adopting during the course of her career – some from her own choosing and others which are forced upon her. The conflicts that arise through having to balance the roles of career woman and home-maker, or through finding oneself forced into an inappropriate role at work, are a major source of stress to many women.

ROLE CONFLICT

The role we adopt at work is affected not only by what we think it should be, but also by:

– our view of ourselves and how well we feel we fit into that role
– others' perceptions of our role
– our perceptions of what others think of us.

Stress occurs when there is conflict between any of the parts of the equation.

Both men and women suffer problems when their view of themselves does not fit comfortably with their view of the ideal manager, or where their managerial role and responsibilities are not clearly defined. Management is still widely perceived to be a male role with the ideal senior executive being a white male graduate who has had an uninterrupted career. Cultures which perpetuate this myth pressurise women into adopting male values and management styles which may sit uncomfortably with the women's natural values and styles, thus increasing female stress and reducing their effectiveness by forcing them to think and work in unnatural ways. Additional stress is caused by worrying how other people view us as a manager.

> My job had previously been done by a man with a dictatorial style. I prefer to lead by example and to treat my staff as a team, but I worry that this will make me seem weak and lacking in authority. I have tried to compromise but still do not feel entirely comfortable.

Day-to-day family responsibilities impinge more on women, even those without children, than they do on men. Not only must we integrate these with our role at work, but we may also have to contend with colleagues who, despite our loyalty, view us as not being 100 per cent committed to the company, just because we are unwilling or unable to work a twelve-hour day.

Practical exercise: Are you suffering from role-conflict?

(1) Do you have a clearly defined view of what your job should entail? Is this written down, agreed and regularly reviewed with your boss?

(2) Do you perceive yourself as handling your job in a different way from that which a man would?

(3) Do you actually know how others perceive you, or do you just think you know?

(4) How much do your roles outside work impinge on your working life, and does this adversely affect your work performance or improve it?

(5) Do you feel stressed when thinking about your role at work and how well you fit into it?

THE TOKEN WOMAN

Despite their official assurances, many companies appoint women to positions not because of their personal merit but because the company wants to be seen to be non-sexist. In its own way, this can be just as harmful both to the individual and to women in general.

> The disadvantages which have been associated with being the token woman include increased performance pressure, visibility, being a test case for future women, isolation and lack of female role models, exclusion from male groups and distortion of women's behaviour by others in order to fit them into pre-existing sex stereotypes.
>
>   (Davidson and Cooper, 1992, p. 84)

A person who is highly visible is under considerable pressure to perform well. Extra effort is needed to avoid making mistakes which will be highlighted, and the token woman faces additional problems when she is expected to attend business meetings, conferences, etc. held at times or locations which impinge on her personal life and responsibilities.

Being the token woman means having to cope with a high degree of isolation. You will have no female peer support, are unlikely to find a more senior woman to act as role model or mentor and may well experience exclusion from the old boy network.

I was proud to be the first woman in our company to be appointed to executive level, but initially found the isolation very stressful. My only female colleagues were subordinates, and there were certain aspects of my work which it would not have been appropriate to discuss with them. I was very conscious that they viewed me as a role model and felt I had to be seen to be fully in control of myself at all times. I was particularly aware that the company's attitude towards senior women would be influenced by the quality, or otherwise, of my performance.

However, there are a number of advantages to be gained:

- high visibility for all your successes and achievements
- being remembered because you stand out in the crowd
- an increase in power, which can be used to your own advantage and to get other women into senior positions.

TIPS

- If you suspect you are being offered a position as a token women, ask yourself:

    - will you be given an equal amount of responsibility and authority to your male peers?
    - how long will it take you to feel comfortable in the position?
    - are the advantages likely to outweigh the disadvantages?
    - what further opportunities is this likely to lead to?

- Once you are appointed:

    - take every opportunity to prove you have been appointed because of your abilities, not your sex. Make sure your achievements can be publicly seen and that you do not minimise your successes by treating them as something routine or allowing others to take the credit
    - make time to find and get to know other women at a similar level in other companies
    - if you make mistakes, let others know that this is because you are human, not Superwoman
    - use your position to convince your employers that many women have the qualities and skills for work at a senior level, and suggest ways in which your company can improve their recruitment, training and promotion procedures and change the underlying culture so that all women get the same chances as men.

BEING A ROLE MODEL

Being viewed as a role model for other women also puts you under more pressure than a man would experience. Even if others do not expect you to be perfect at all times, you will yourself feel the need to constantly project an image of not only being good at your job but also of being a woman who is good at that job. When you make mistakes, you will feel that you are not only letting yourself down, but are also letting down all the other women in the company.

You may experience additional calls on your time, such as being invited to talk to women's groups or being asked by individuals for your support and help. If you agree, you eat into your working time; if you refuse, you will alienate the women below you.

The pressure on the few is easing as more women get appointed to senior positions, but when being offered a post which will put you in the position of a role model, think carefully about all the implications and ensure you are prepared to cope with these additional pressures. The benefits are, like those for the token woman, high visibility which could lead to further opportunities – an advantage not likely to be so readily available to a man in a similar post.

TIPS

- If you receive a lot of requests to speak about the role of the senior women manager, build up a list of women in similar positions and suggest that you handle these on a rota basis, to spread the load.
- Ask for your expenses, at least, to be paid. Many groups offer a speaker's fee as well as expenses – by charging, you emphasise the value of your time.

INAPPROPRIATE ROLES

Whereas male managers tend to have one role – that of the traditional, stereotyped manager, there are many different roles that women can adopt. Not all of these are appropriate, and some may lead you into further difficulties.

Some women have made a bad name for themselves and for women in general by taking advantage of their sex in inappropriate ways:

> I once had a department head whose behaviour made me feel ashamed to be female – she acted as the 'poor little woman' and had all the men running round after her doing any job which she did not want to do herself. It was all an act – she was as hard as nails underneath and it didn't take them long to find this out. It took the rest of us ages to live down the bad name she gave to women.

The mother confessor

The assumption that women are more caring than men about other people often leads to women taking on the role of the caring, nurturing mother confessor who provides a shoulder to cry on for anyone who needs it. This is time-consuming and emotionally tiring, can adversely affect your own job performance and leads to conflict with the traditional view of the executive role. It may put you in a position of power through receiving confidential information not available to the male manager, but this in itself can cause you strain because you cannot make overt use of information which has been given to you in confidence.

> With the exception of female supervisors, the majority of women managers maintained that positively resisting the imposition of the mother role at work was a necessary tactic, if one wanted to be taken seriously as a 'manager'.
>
> (Davidson and Cooper, 1992, p. 91)

The departmental mascot

This is similar to the company mascot role in which the token woman finds herself. It often arises where your bosses and peers are of the 'old school' and don't take you seriously, but protect you, pat you on the head and tell you 'not to worry about men's problems'. Male sales representatives are particularly guilty of such behaviour, going to great lengths to show what they deem to be the old-fashioned courtesy that they feel is women's due, not realising that their behaviour is patronising and demeaning.

The departmental tea lady

Women managers often find themselves being asked to do domestic-type jobs that their male colleagues are not expected to do, such as making the tea or photocopying. This arises from the unenlightened male manager's view of women as the home-makers or secretaries – if you fail to enlighten them on the proper role of the manager, you will only reinforce their view. Firmly resist any such inappropriate requests.

The bridesmaid

Making yourself indispensable to your boss may ensure that you continue to have employment, but could also ensure that you miss out on promotion.

> My boss always gave me glowing performance reports but said he felt I was not yet ready for promotion. Then a colleague told me she had overheard him saying that the real reason was because he would never be able to find anyone as good to replace me.

The seductress

Attractive women who play on their sex to progress their career build up nothing but trouble for themselves. A mild flirtation to pass the time of day may be just a bit of fun at the start, but it could be taken seriously by the recipient, and onlookers ripe for a bit of office gossip will quickly jump to the conclusion that you are sharing more than just a lunch.

Another problem is being viewed by others as a sex object when nothing is further from your mind. You may have difficulty in getting promotion because of a fear that you will cause problems with male employees, customers or suppliers. Alternatively, your employers may try to push you into jobs, such as a customer-facing role, where they think your sex will benefit the company.

TIPS

- When men pay you compliments about your appearance, accept them gracefully but don't let them make an issue about it. If they make unwanted comments, try turning it into a serious conversation about clothes generally.
- Be aware of the chemistry between you and your male colleagues and the effect it can have on your work and career. There will always be some people with whom you 'click', but keep all your work relationships on a business, rather than a personal footing wherever possible.
- If you receive unwanted approaches, tell the man firmly that you are not interested.
- Don't take things to the other extreme and become 'hard' – if you totally submerge your femininity you risk being called the Iron Maiden or similar derogatory names, which is just as harmful.

THE FEMINIST

Are you keeping your head below the parapet because you don't want to be labelled a feminist?

(Joanna Foster)

Why is the term 'aggressive' always used about women who challenge things?

(Sumita Dutta SIA)

Collins Shorter English Dictionary (1973 edition) describes feminism as 'the doctrine that maintains the equality of the sexes, advocacy of women's rights'. Unfortunately, many people equate the term with extremism and anti-male practices, thus women who stand up for their own rights and those of women generally risk being labelled militant and as trouble-makers by those who see feminism as threatening or who use the term as an excuse for refusing to consider the female point of view. Such hostility may come from both men and women.

Once you have been labelled an extremist, it will be very difficult for you to get people to listen rationally to your views. Striking the right balance between inaction and extremism in such an emotive area is not easy; there will be many times when you have to stop yourself saying something which would escalate the immediate situation out of all proportion.

For this reason, many women avoid the word 'feminist'. Some deny supporting women's rights or become scared of doing or saying anything which might earn them this label, thus helping to perpetuate the male culture and values and the causes of female stress.

We will never gain equal rights and protect our integrity if we continue to compromise ourselves by accepting the male value system as the only appropriate one. We need to understand and interpret the existing system, clarify our own cultures and values and continue striving to change the culture so that our values can be integrated alongside those of men. We can only do this successfully if we find a way to avoid being labelled an extremist. Your aim is to win the support of others (of both sexes), gain the co-operation of the people with whom you are negotiating, and achieve positive action.

TIPS

- Laugh off any inappropriate labels, or ask the labeller to define what they mean by the label and how they feel it applies to you. Take care not to become aggressive or defensive.
- Seek practical, rather than confrontational or accusatorial, ways of changing the general culture.
- Network with other women for mutual support.
- When facing a specific situation which you need to redress:
  - avoid direct confrontation at all times – seek more subtle ways to redress the situation
  - carefully consider all aspects rather than jumping into immediate action. Allowing yourself a cooling-off period will help you to assess the situation more objectively, canvass support and properly plan the best way forward
  - find out all the facts that you can. Is the situation due to overall company policy or culture, or has it been caused by localised attitudes or a local situation?
  - think carefully about your own reactions. Is the situation really as bad as you think, or are you allowing your emotions to colour your judgement?
  - find out what other people think about the situation but avoid setting up clandestine meetings which could be labelled subversive
  - collect as much hard evidence as you can to show that your view is reasonable and in the general interest of the organization and its employees. Obtain facts from other organizations to support your case
  - seek the support of as many people as possible – both men and women. Look particularly for supporters in positions of authority and influence who will actively back you up.
  - keep a tight rein on your emotions during discussions. Aim to be seen as reasonable and co-operative, and depersonalise the debate as much as possible. Avoid using threats such as calling in the union or higher management – you may have to take such action if you can't reach agreement, but keep things as low-key as possible at the initial stage.

If you handle the situation properly you should be able to negotiate an acceptable solution without being labelled militant or feminist, and your success will help boost both your own self-confidence and the respect that others have for you.

SHOULD WOMEN ACT LIKE MEN?

If you can't beat them, join them.

In the past, those women who made it to the top often did so because they submerged their femininity, projecting an image which would fit the stereotyped view of the successful male executive – ambitious, assertive, single-minded, totally committed to their company and a full-time career, task-orientated, a dynamic driving force, an autocratic leader, willing to work long hours. They wore formal suits in dark or subdued colours, which would not stand out against the suits of their male colleagues, and were careful to do nothing to draw attention to their sex.

Happily, enough women have now demonstrated their executive abilities for us to be able to move away from the 'more of a man than a man' role. This has been helped by changes in thinking about the most effective company structure and management style – the move towards greater emphasis on individual flexibility, team-building and ethics/values means that many companies now realise that the traditional male-based executive role and values are out of date. Instead of seeking managers who fit the traditional mould, employers have started actively looking for a variety of different management styles.

Women now have the freedom to retain their femininity within the boundaries of the job they do and still demonstrate that they are achievers and can produce the required results just as effectively as a man. Indeed, adopting the male 'macho' role is likely to be less, not more, effective for today's female executive, but we may still have to work at convincing certain individuals of the effectiveness of female managerial styles.

CHOOSING YOUR ROLE

Selecting the role most appropriate to yourself and your job is not easy. There will be many influencing factors – the requirements of the job, the culture of the company and the way your bosses and peers expect you to act, your career aspirations, private life responsibilities and your personality.

Practical exercise: Which role(s) have you adopted?

(1)   High visibility.
(2)   Isolated from other women/supportive men/female role models.
(3)   A position of power and influence.
(4)   An expert in your field.
(5)   A role model for other women.
(6)   Someone reliable who can always be depended upon.
(7)   Welcoming a challenge; willing to take risks.
(8)   A warm, caring person always happy to give time to others.
(9)   More concerned about what others think of you than how you think about yourself.

(10)   Making use of your feminine traits to gain admiration/advancement.
(11)   Allowing others to use you in ways inappropriate to your position/to patronise you.
(12)   Giving more importance to the task than to people.
(13)   The ever-dependable right-hand assistant.
(14)   Totally submerging your femininity – the 'invisible' person.
(15)   More like a man than a man.
(16)   A militant feminist.
(17)   Achieving your career aspirations at the expense of others.
(18)   Giving priority to your work at the expense of your personal life.
(19)   Giving priority to your personal life at the expense of your career.
(20)   Suffering confusion/stress because of conflict between the role with which you feel comfortable and the role you think you should play.
(21)   Suffering confusion/stress because of conflict between your career and personal life.

Re-assess all the factors relating to your career and yourself as an individual and decide whether you need to work on adopting a more appropriate role.

TIPS

- Regularly think about/re-assess the role you have adopted.
- Do not allow the job/other people to push you into a role with which you will never feel fully comfortable.
- Make a positive effort to adapt your naturally preferred role to the needs of the job/your career aspirations.

MENTORING

Mentoring is a work relationship between two people, one of whom acts as counsellor or patron to the other. The mentor is usually a more senior person who can use their experience, skills and position to help the other settle into their job or progress their career; although this may sound like a one-way relationship, both parties should be able to gain extensively from it.

Men have made use of informal mentoring for many years; indeed the master craftsman–apprentice relationship could be said to be a form of mentoring. More recently, recognition of mentoring as a formal management technique and career development method has been adopted by UK companies as part of their standard culture. Mentoring can be between the same sexes or different sexes, though many women prefer a female mentor.

Formal mentoring

Companies such as IBM, BP, BT and an increasing number of public sector organizations have set up formal systems to help develop new recruits, younger employees, graduate entrants, women, ethnic minorities, disabled people, etc. Identifying high-flyers early in their career and managing their development is a form of formal mentoring used to improve the calibre of a company's future management.

Individuals benefiting from such career-development systems are not usually allocated a personal mentor but they gain access to a wider range of experience, better training and self-development and properly structured career-planning.

Another form of mentoring adopted by some employers is to provide employees with access to a career counsellor, either in-house or externally.

A true mentoring arrangement where individuals have their own personal mentor is difficult to set up under a formal system, mainly because its success depends to a great extent on the personalities of the individuals and the degree to which they are able to interact successfully. Mentoring involves a high degree of emotional commitment and empathy on both sides, and allocation of mentors by the employer rather than allowing individuals to choose their own mentor can result in mismatches. In the best case, this does nothing more than waste both parties' time; in the worst case it does untold damage to the self-confidence and career opportunities of both partners.

> The mentor I was allocated was a more senior woman in Personnel. I already knew her slightly, but when we met to discuss my career I got the impression she was merely playing at mentoring so as to be seen to do so for her own benefit. She made no attempt to empathise with my feelings – instead of giving me the moral support I needed she spent most of her time criticising my outlook.

Formal mentoring has the advantage of official recognition, thus individuals can take time out from their work to discuss matters with their mentoring partner. Also, the mentor may get official recognition for their mentoring skills which could be of use in progressing their own career.

Case study

Over the last couple of years, the London Borough of Waltham Forest's Women's Unit has been piloting a formal mentoring scheme. Although final evaluation had not taken place at the time of writing this, a number of useful points can be learned from their experience.

The Women's Unit began by circulating a leaflet asking female employees interested in becoming mentors to contact the unit. Potential mentors were given training, firstly to learn about the concept of mentoring and then a two-day session to teach them counselling, and similar skills. Having trained about thirty women as mentors, the unit circulated a leaflet offering mentoring services to individual women. Potential mentees were asked to state their department, particular areas of interest and the type of mentor they would like (such as a returner, parent, disabled woman, black woman, lesbian, etc.) and the unit then matched them up with a mentor meeting those requirements. Participants were granted a small amount of working time each month to meet with their partner.

Initially, only a very few mentees applied, so the unit issued a leaflet which more fully explained the system and benefits and the take-up rate improved, although by that time some potential mentors were no longer available or interested. To maintain privacy, partners were not asked to provide feedback on the system but their views will be sought when the pilot is formally evaluated.

Sue Hancock of the Women's Unit feels that the initial low take-up by mentees might have been due to a lack of understanding about mentoring, a fear that by officially requesting a mentor a woman was admitting to having problems or needing help, or that there was little requirement for a formal scheme because women were finding their own informal mentors. She feels in retrospect that, rather than sending out a leaflet, it might have been better to have held a lunchtime meeting for potential mentees as a group, to explain the system, answer individual questions, provide group support for individuals and ascertain the extent to which they had already found their own informal mentor.

Formal systems require:

- research into requirements, to establish whether or not employees need/would benefit from a formal system
- professional training for potential mentors
- detailed explanations and advice to potential mentees, preferably in group sessions
- individuals being given a degree of freedom in selecting their partner
- partners being officially allowed time during the working day for mentoring
- effective monitoring at each stage to establish the effectiveness and identify any problem areas.

Informal mentoring

The most successful mentoring arrangements are often those initiated informally between individuals with mutual feelings of empathy, respect and desire to interact. The arrangement may develop naturally, or it may be sought deliberately by one or the other. Usually the most junior partner (the mentee) will be the person to take the initiative as it is they who feel the need of advice, but the arrangement may also be initiated by the mentor who wants to help increase the number of women at her own level or who spots someone needing their support.

The benefits of mentoring

Mentoring should be two-sided with both parties having something to give and gain. Unless an extremely good relationship is developed, a one-sided arrangement may deteriorate to the point that the person not gaining anything begins to feel put-upon and resentful. A good mentoring arrangement is similar to (and may well develop from or into) a close personal friendship, with give and take on both sides.

The mentee gains:

- access to greater experience, a wider range of contacts and knowledge, different perspectives
- a chance to tap into the power and influence of their mentor
- a sounding board for their ideas
- a role model
- moral support and encouragement
- a shoulder to cry on/someone with whom to let off steam
- help in clarifying their image, role and aspirations
- an impartial but caring opinion
- practical help in progressing their career
- improved motivation
- an opportunity to develop improved communication and interpersonal skills
- a better understanding of themselves and their abilities and skills
- increased self-confidence
- a champion.

   The mentor gains:

- a loyal supporter and friend
- a sounding board for their own ideas
- an opportunity to re-assess their own image, aspirations and plans
- an opportunity to practise and refine their communication, listening, and counselling skills
- access to knowledge and contacts, particularly if the mentee works in a different department or company
- someone with whom they can themselves let off steam
- access to a potential future team member (many senior managers actively recruit their teams from the people they already know and trust).

   I had help for a short time from a mentor some years ago. She gave me very helpful tips on the best way to phrase local authority job applications, and I found her assistance and support invaluable.
                            (Sue Hancock, London Borough of Waltham Forest)

Being an effective mentor

It is not enough merely to want to help someone. Effective mentoring involves a great deal of skill, not least in human psychology. To avoid possible conflict, it is best not to mentor one of your own immediate staff.

An effective mentor:

- is a good listener
- understands the difference between counselling and advising
- is able to quickly establish rapport with their mentee
- respects and understands their mentee
- acts as a sounding board, allowing their mentee to think out loud
- guides the mentee to find solutions for themselves, rather than telling them what they should do
- has the knowledge, experience and contacts to which their mentee needs access
- is able to influence others who can be of help to their mentee
- understands the mentee's job and the culture and structure of their company/department
- will not feel threatened by their mentee
- can think through situations and analyse them dispassionately
- is willing/able to give the time and commitment needed
- truly cares about their mentee as a person but avoids getting over-involved emotionally in their situation
- commands respect and is totally trustworthy
- is perceptive, patient and enthusiastic
- is willing and able to speak the truth, but in a constructive, not destructive, way
- is able to understand and relate to the mentee's personality, background and lifestyle
- provides moral support and encouragement, constructive criticism and advice, and practical help.

Pitfalls to avoid

Mentoring is not the answer to every career problem and it is important not to rely on it totally. A bad mentoring arrangement will do more harm than good – if you get into a bad relationship, end it and make alternative arrangements as soon as possible. Other pitfalls to watch out for:

Mentor:

- lacks the necessary counselling skills, patience, understanding and interpersonal skills
- instructs the mentee in what to do rather than helping them decide on the best way forward
- has insufficient experience, knowledge or contacts to provide the required practical help

- has insufficient time to spare the mentee or has to cancel discussions at short notice
- lacks influence; is thought badly of by their contacts
- does not understand the mentee's situation/work responsibilities/ company or departmental culture
- lacks understanding of the mentee's personal situation/outlook/ cultural background
- has a close relationship with a person causing the mentee problems (though this can sometimes be used to advantage)
- is the mentee's direct supervisor, which may cause a conflict of interest or create problems with the rest of their team
- is reluctant to help the mentee progress because of a desire to retain the relationship/the mentee's services
- lacks the required personal commitment
- feels threatened by mentee ('If I help her progress, she might take over my job')
- is motivated by a desire to gain glory for themselves
- uses the discussion sessions mainly to discuss their own problems
- lacks discretion/fails to maintain confidentiality.

Mentee:

- is reluctant to be fully open with their mentor because they fear being thought badly of/not meeting their expectations
- becomes too dependent on their mentor and cannot function without their support
- uses the relationship to 'get one up on' their peers.

General:

- lack of empathy/rapport between the partners; personality conflicts
- lack of respect on one or both side(s)
- close relationship of partners causes resentment/fear in others (partners assumed to be 'ganging up' on others)
- relationship causes gossip (particularly if partners are of different sexes)
- age/seniority gap between partners is too great
- difficulty in getting manager's agreement to the time needed for mentoring (in informal arrangements).

Male versus female mentors

Most women seem to prefer a female mentor; the reasons given include:

- do not have to maintain a pretence, can let my hair down
- understands if I want to cry
- easier to establish close personal rapport
- less likelihood of harmful gossip
- female mentor shares my outlook/approach to work/management style.

The main problem cited is the lack of women at a more senior level available to act as mentors.

Many women report having benefited from informal mentoring by a male boss who helped encourage and train them for higher-grade work – these are actions which should be standard management practice of any boss.

TIPS: Finding a suitable mentor

- If your organization has no formal mentoring system, you may like to suggest to the management that they consider setting one up.
- If looking to set up your own arrangements informally, study the above list of skills/attributes required. Look for a mentor who will be able to fully understand your situation but is not themselves too closely involved in it. Choose someone you respect and trust and with whom you already have, or can quickly build up, a rapport.
- You may initially prefer to begin the relationship without mentioning mentoring as such, by asking your selected person for some advice. Once you are sure you have chosen the right person, either gradually develop the relationship on an informal basis, or put it on a more formal basis by asking them if they are willing to act as your mentor and then jointly deciding how you are going to organize it. Beware of assuming that the other person knows they are your mentor if you have not actually agreed this with them.
- If you find you have chosen the wrong person, don't panic – identify what it is about them that is wrong and use the experience to help you select someone more suitable.
- If there is no-one suitable within your own organization, look outside it using your business or social contacts. If you choose a mentor from a totally different background or in a different type of organization or field of work, make sure they will be able to properly understand your situation, otherwise their advice might be inappropriate.

NETWORKING

The men's business club is not a set of rules but a way of thinking.

Networking is the female equivalent of the informal old boy network – it provides information, contacts and support and is invaluable to the female manager or potential manager. There are two types of women's networks – informal and formal.

Networking provides:

- a forum for exchanging information and ideas
- opportunities for personal and business development
- facilities for establishing contacts beyond your immediate circle
- awareness about business and personal issues.

Informal networks

As for men, informal networks consist of a group of friends with mutual interests, either work or social, who meet whenever they feel like it. The group may be large or small and members may work for the same or different employers. The get-togethers, often held over a drink or a meal, provide opportunities for sharing ideas and knowledge in an informal setting. If you are having career problems, a friend from your informal network may be the ideal sounding board or mentor; a group discussion about your problem with people you trust will generate many different ideas and help cheer you up and remotivate you. Sharing the problem with your friends may not give you the solution but their support and encouragement will help you get the problem in perspective.

The benefits of informal networking:

- set up by friends with mutual interests
- times/venues for get-togethers are flexible
- plenty of time to talk to others
- relaxing, informal atmosphere
- opportunities for sharing information, ideas, contacts
- mutual support gained from friends
- no need to 'maintain appearances' (can let your hair down with people who know and understand you)
- may be based near home rather than work
- 'entry' is through invitation from an existing member so new members know at least one person when they 'join'
- no financial commitment such as an annual membership fee.

Drawbacks are:

- no particular focus – may degenerate into gossip session
- size may be self-limiting; group may remain inward-looking and form a clique to which newcomers are not welcome
- no structured opportunity for learning new management skills or gaining career advice/information
- may be an unsuitable forum for admitting to your problems (not wanting to show yourself up in front of friends)
- friends may be from different work background – may not understand your situation
- locally based so will lose touch if moving away.

Formal networks

The number and variety of formal women's networks both in the UK and internationally is increasing rapidly. The networks are usually set up and managed by a committee or steering group, and may be for members in a specific company, a specific field of work or for women generally. Most charge a fee for membership or events and hold organised meetings on a regular basis; larger networks also publish a regular newsletter. Meetings usually have a specific theme with speakers or facilitators plus time for socialising/networking; most networks hold their meetings in a central location outside office hours.

Because most formal networks are run on a voluntary basis, it is often difficult to obtain their contact address (which may change as the officers change) unless you know someone who is already a member. A selection of networks and their addresses is given in the Further Information section – to find additional networks, ask around among your existing contacts or look out for a mention in the press or professional journals.

The benefits of formal networks are:

- members have mutual areas of interest
- opportunities for sharing information, ideas, contacts, for developing business and personal awareness
- meetings focus on specific topics
- structured opportunities for developing business and personal skills and career advice/information
- access to a wide range of contacts
- forum for getting your skills and abilities widely known
- opportunity for meeting role models and mentors
- larger networks are nationally based with local groups, so are location-independent.

The drawbacks are:

- times/venues may be unsuitable
- lack of time (in structured meetings) to chat to others
- atmosphere less informal (may feel the need to project a professional image rather than letting your hair down)
- attending on your own initially requires courage
- annual membership fee might be high

Do networks increase women's isolation from men?

Several women have told me that they would not join a women's network because they fear these help to create/perpetuate the 'them and us' barriers between men and women. Men with a good informal network system cannot understand the need for formal networks for women; others view women's networks merely as a forum for talking about babies and family life or suspect they revolve around militant or subversive activities. Fortunately, the people that feel this way are in the minority.

Although equality issues are always high on the agenda in women's networks, so too are management techniques, stress-coping tips and balancing work and family life. Many men I have spoken to think formal networks are a great idea for both sexes and wish they had access to a similar forum. It is not unusual for men to be allowed or invited to attend a women's meeting – this helps not only to educate them about the nature

TIPS

- Attending a formal network meeting on your own for the first time can be daunting. Most meetings start with refreshments and time to circulate – this is your opportunity to get to know people. Telephone the organizer beforehand and tell them you would like to be introduced to a few members. When you arrive, ask for the organizer by name and introduce yourself; they should then introduce you to one or two other members. If there is no-one to introduce you, look for another woman who appears to be on her own and introduce yourself to her – it is probable that she, too, knows no-one and will more than welcome your advance.
- If attending with a friend or friends, ensure you circulate and talk to other members.
- You will only get out of the network what you put in. Take an active part in discussions and training seminars; use the network to practise and refine your interpersonal, presentation, etc. skills; consolidate your relationship with the people you meet and gradually extend your circle of contacts. Give as much help and support to the people you meet as that which you receive yourself.
- The best way to build up contacts is to join the organizing committee or help run a specific event. The time you invest will be well worthwhile.
- Avoid joining too many networks and thus not having time to attend each on a regular basis. Try out several and pick the one(s) you find most useful.

of women's networks but also allows them to hear and gain a greater understanding of women's views. A minority of women feel resentful if men attend or are a guest speaker – I personally am only too happy to welcome those men who support equal opportunities, understand and support women and can help to educate less-enlightened males.

6

BALANCING WORK AND HOME

The holistic approach – The single, childless female manager – The married female manager – The working mother – The carer – Setting life goals – Family-friendly working practices – Career breaks – Coping with conflict

Working women have dual management responsibilities – those of the work and the home – and home responsibilities are more time-consuming for most women than for men. Increased work responsibility and pressure as we move up the ladder adds to the stress caused by having to integrate our dual roles and find the time to adequately discharge all our responsibilities.

> Paid work affects housework in different ways for men and women. As women increase the time they spend in paid employment, they do not shed an equivalent amount of domestic work. Roughly, for every extra hour of paid work, women do half-an-hour less domestic work.
>
> (Hewitt, 1993, p. 57)

This inequality adds to our career problems and is one reason for an increasing number of dedicated career women staying single, getting divorced, delaying having children or opting to remain childless. It is however possible for all of us to achieve a satisfactory balance, though some compromise will inevitably be needed.

THE HOLISTIC APPROACH

Work and personal life inter-relate, however much men may compartmentalise them. Women prefer the holistic approach, treating their career as an integrated part of their life and viewing the whole as a balance of work, home and play.

The drawback is that we never completely switch off from our personal responsibilities – often having to fit the shopping into our lunchbreak or scheduling work commitments around carer responsibilities. The benefit is that we become adept at balancing a wide variety of responsibilities – a skill which is of immense value as an effective management technique at work.

This difference in outlook helps perpetuate untrue, but harmful, assumptions about a woman's ability to hold down a responsible job:

Women will always give their family priority over work.

It is unfair and unrealistic to expect a woman to have the strength and energy to be a full-time career person as well as a wife and mother.

A woman manager can never give her complete attention and energy to her work.

TIP

● Whenever you hear this sort of remark, make a point of giving examples of how the female holistic approach makes a woman manager more, not less, effective than a man.

Older male executives with non-working wives base their assumptions on their own experience and lifestyle and may have difficulty understanding how a home can be well run with both partners working full time. They forget that many non-working wives spend a great deal of their time on voluntary or community activities whilst continuing to run the home satisfactorily.

As later generations of men with working wives take over the senior positions, attitudes are changing. This is helped by the increasing number of men with executive-level wives whose career is as important as, or more important than, their partner's. Life values for men as well as women are changing, with greater emphasis being given to the overall quality of life – men are beginning to adopt the holistic view and seek quality time to spend with their family instead of concentrating on work to the exclusion of all else. The dual income which working couples enjoy allows the husband the freedom to reject long working hours or refuse relocation if he wishes.

THE SINGLE, CHILDLESS FEMALE MANAGER

Although some women choose to remain single and childless in order to progress their career particularly during their twenties and early thirties, most do so because it suits them as a person – the fact that they will face fewer career barriers forms only a part of their decision.

The 'average' single person, whether male or female, is viewed as:

- having fewer domestic ties and responsibilities
- mobile and willing to relocate to progress their career
- dedicated to their career
- willing to work longer/less social hours.

Employers may be more willing to invest time and money in developing the career of a woman who remains single, because they do not fear she will become pregnant or need to relocate because of her husband's job.

As single people become both older and more senior, they notice a number of disadvantages:

- being viewed as abnormal, an oddity
- lack of emotional and domestic support – loneliness, needing a 'wife'
- not fitting in to the executive entertaining/socialising scene which expects managers to be one of a couple.

THE MARRIED FEMALE MANAGER

In respect to organizational attitude, the married male manager tends to be viewed as an asset, whereas the married female managers are a liability.

(Davidson and Cooper, 1992, p. 133)

Married women frequently face interview questions such as 'How soon do you plan to have children?', 'What effect will your children have on your work?' or 'If your husband's employer wanted him to move to another part of the country, whose career would take precedence?'. Such questions are discriminatory unless also asked of men, but it is difficult to take issue with a company's equal opportunities practices when you are in the middle of an interview, without adversely affecting your chances of getting the job.

Looking at it from the employers' viewpoint one can understand their wish to appoint the person who is going to give them the best value for money. They are looking for an assurance that a woman's domestic circumstances will not in any way interfere with her work performance.

TIPS

- Be prepared in advance for such questions and decide how you are going to answer them – picture yourself in the interviewer's position and think about the sort of response you would be seeking.
- Avoid becoming aggressive or defensive – either politely assure the interviewer that your personal life will not adversely affect your work performance and leave it at that, or explain to them the arrangements you have for coping with your domestic responsibilities.
- If you feel it necessary to comment on the line of questioning, make sure you do this in a way which will not label you as a trouble maker.

On the face of it, the childless married woman has the best of both worlds – she has a partner to support her emotionally and share the domestic chores, is likely to have fewer financial worries because of a dual income and has no children to detract from her career performance or prospects.

In practice, the majority of married women still face more problems than men, with most feeling that they take on a far wider range of responsibilities than men, though women who work part-time are more likely to feel satisfied with managing the home and family life than are full-time workers. The problems married women face include:

- encountering employers who expect them to have children at some stage in the future
- taking on the greater share of the domestic burden at the end of a long working day, with the resultant drain of energy
- feeling guilty if domestic chores remain undone
- conflict with their partner over the split of domestic responsibilities or conflict between career and family priorities
- taking on the greater share of caring responsibilities for both sets of older parents.

Relationships with your partner

Instead of the traditional dominant husband – subordinate wife relationship, an equal balance is needed where both sides understand and accept their partner's work-role and responsibilities, particularly as the woman progresses her career and takes on greater responsibilities and more time-consuming commitments. Disputes arise when one or other partner views their career as more important than their partner's career. Conflict can also arise when the woman:

- has a more senior position and/or earns more than her partner
- has to work late, attend residential conferences or training courses or bring work home
- wants to socialise with her male colleagues after work so as to remain an equal part of the team
- wants to network with other women outside working hours
- feels the majority of domestic chores are her responsibility.

Conflict also arises from:

- partners giving precedence to their career over their personal life, to suddenly find they have no time for each other, few shared interests and are drifting apart
- wanting children but needing the wife's income or not wishing to jeopardise the wife's career
- one or other being required to relocate to retain their job or gain advancement.

Does the 'new man' exist?

It is sometimes suggested that behind every successful high-powered businesswoman there is a 'new man', who supports his wife in her career by performing an equal share of housework and childcare. But

are families really changing? Does the new man really exist? Research suggests that he does, but that he remains a fairly rare breed.
(Davidson and Cooper, 1992, p. 141)

Even though my husband will happily help me round the house, he only does so when I ask him to. I resent the fact that it is always me who has to think about whether the ironing needs doing or what food needs buying for the week.

One solution is to hire domestic help for a few hours a week. A good cleaner does not cost a great deal – the main problem is finding someone you can trust. Ask your friends and contacts for recommendations or use a reputable agency. Interview prospective cleaners in the same way that you would interview a prospective employee, brief them fully on the work you want done and set an initial trial period. Don't be afraid to dismiss them if you are not happy with their work. The savings you make in time and stress may well outweigh the financial cost.

TIPS

- Do not wear yourself out both physically and emotionally by trying to be Superwoman. Decide where your priorities lie and organize your life round these. How important is it to you that the carpets get vacuumed every week?
- Talk to your partner to ensure you understand each other's career responsibilities and aspirations and overall life values and priorities.
- Discuss the domestic responsibilities and jointly agree the way in which these will be shared – use this as an opportunity to practise your negotiating skills. Choose a time when you both feel relaxed and are unlikely to get into an argument. Ask your partner to take responsibility for specific tasks, so you do not have to shoulder every domestic responsibility yourself.
- If you find yourself feeling stressed because your partner does not place the importance you do on domestic matters, ask yourself which actually causes you the most stress – frequently getting into dispute with your partner, accepting his standards but feeling guilty, or doing the chores yourself? You may find it less stressful and tiring in the long run to accept without resentment the fact that you have different values, and just get on with the chores yourself if you feel they need doing.
- Consider hiring domestic help for a few hours each week or using a commercial firm for a full spring-clean twice a year.

My first husband always left me to work out our finances. I resented this because it was an additional pressure on me and I did not see why I should always have to take the initiative and responsibility. We had rows about it every month. My current husband has a similar attitude, but I have learned to accept his outlook, have realised that I actually prefer having financial control myself, and just get on with the task. It now causes me no stress at all.

Work and private life are interlinked – what affects one inevitably affects the other. If work problems adversely affect your home life, your personal relationships can deteriorate to the point where they in turn adversely affect your working life, and vice versa. Women prefer to share their work problems with their partner, using them as a sounding board or shoulder to cry on but also often taking their work frustrations out on them. Men tend to keep their work problems to themselves, becoming morose and emotionally isolated. It is important that both sides understand the other's personality and the way they react to stress, so that they can give help and support in the most effective way.

TIPS

- If your partner becomes stressed and emotionally isolated from you but refuses to discuss their problem or denies that they have a problem, continually asking him what the matter is will only make things worse. Instead, demonstrate that you still love and fully support him, and allow him to solve his problem in his own way or discuss it with you when he feels the time is right.
- If his attitude causes you serious stress, tell him about the effect it has on you but make it clear that you respect his right to keep his problems to himself.
- If you find yourself taking your work frustrations out on your partner, be aware of the effect this is likely to have on him and your relationship.

THE WORKING MOTHER

Contraception and improvements in the career opportunities open to women, modern social attitudes and employment legislation have resulted in a greater number of women actively seeking to combine a career and motherhood. Women are delaying childbirth until they have established their career, and the amount of time they spend out of employment has reduced considerably with many mothers returning to their full-time career shortly after having children. However, combining work and motherhood inevitably adds to women's problems. We suffer:

- increased responsibility, calls on our time and emotional and physical pressure/stress
- feelings of guilt because we are unable to give either our work or our children our total time and attention
- stereotyping by employers who assume us to be incapable of meeting the full commitments of our job
- restricted career opportunities due either to employers' attitudes or family commitments.

The number of lone mothers with children under the age of 16 has increased dramatically in the last decade. Forty-two per cent of all lone mothers are aged 25–34 years; just over 10 per cent of mothers in the 35–44 age group and 14 per cent in the 45–59 age group are single. Fathers constitute around 10 per cent of single parents. Single fathers are much more likely to be employed than are single mothers; single mothers are much less likely to be working, and are generally less qualified, than are married or co-habiting mothers, although around one in five single mothers have qualifications at A-level or above (Employment Department statistics).

Single mothers, whether separated, divorced, widowed or never married, face enormous problems in trying to find work, not least because of employer attitudes and lack of adequate childcare schemes. Despite the government stressing the importance of the traditional family unit, it is vital that adequate practical solutions to the problems of childcare are found so as to enable employers to make use of the vast pool of female experience and skills which is available.

Both the government and employers are increasingly recognising the value of meeting the needs of the working mother, and the importance of managed maternity breaks, childcare schemes and family-friendly working practices are widely publicised. In 1993, the government announced plans to spend £45 million over three years to help create out-of-school schemes for the children of working parents and the last few years have seen a sharp increase in training schemes for returners. However, despite the publicity, active campaigning and such initiatives, discrimination against working mothers still abounds. Childcare provision is expensive, the recent introduction of stringent EC regulations put some childcare providers out of business and increased the fees that others have to charge, the Child Support Act has created additional problems and worries for single mothers, and the recent recession drastically reduced the number of jobs available. It is obvious that there is still a long way to go before the needs of working mothers are fully met. Indeed, as I am writing this, the government are considering how they plan to handle the revised maternity arrangements laid down in the EC's Social Chapter, which will in autumn 1994 abolish the length-of-service requirements for pregnant women and may lead to reduced state compensation paid to employers. It is suggested that British business may have to foot an £80 million bill for improved maternity benefits, thus making employers even more reluctant to employ women who might require maternity leave at some point in their career.

Combining work and childcare

The working mother has a number of options:

- full-time childcare through either a company, local authority or private scheme, or through family, friends or a paid employee such as a nanny or au pair
- part-time childcare combined with part-time work
- after-school care during term time, combined with term-time working or temporary childcare

– working from home (though this on its own is not the total solution).

A small but increasing number of fathers are giving up work to look after their children whilst their wife pursues her career. Society in general is coming to view this as fully acceptable, but at a local level both father and mother may find themselves facing disapproval and criticism, not least from their immediate family members.

Good quality childcare at an affordable price is in scarce supply. Commuting to a company crèche at your place of work with babies or young children is not always practical. Local childcare may prevent you from staying late at work in an emergency; a child who is taken ill may prevent you from attending work, children at school may necessitate you working locally or prevent you from relocating. Whatever the situation, a working mother suffers additional drains on her finances, will always find herself pulled in two directions at once and may be forced to make a choice between progressing her career and meeting her parental responsibilities.

TIPS

- Ensure you know your employment rights, particularly with respect to maternity leave and job security.
- Research the alternative options open to working mothers, and particularly the schemes and attitudes adopted by family-friendly employers.
- Obtain the advice and support of national and local groups such as the Working Mothers' Association, the various childcare organizations, and mothers working in your company.
- Carefully consider and decide on your career and parenting objectives and priorities.
- If you have a sympathetic employer, discuss your maternity plans and career aspirations with them to explore the best way to meet the needs of both sides. Tell them about the practices other companies have introduced and stress your continuing commitment to your employer.
- Get your older children to take responsibility for helping in the home – this is good training for them.
- Seek professional help if you feel you are being discriminated against because you have or are planning children.
- Campaign for tax relief on childcare costs.

Maternity breaks

All employers must by law give the statutory minimum maternity facilities to employees who meet the legal specifications about length of service and hours of work (length-of-service requirements are due to be abolished in autumn 1994), and many larger organizations offer more than the statutory minimum. Ensure that you know your statutory rights and arrange for your employer to keep you in touch with company developments while you are away from work.

Having a member of staff go on maternity leave creates problems for the immediate manager and often causes bad feeling. You can help protect your relationship with your boss by being aware of their problems and talking the situation through with them.

THE CARER

People are living longer and state care for the elderly is being reduced, throwing the responsibility for care on to relatives. Invariably this burden falls on women, who often have to take on the main share of looking after their partner's relatives as well as their own. Many successful career women are being forced to curtail their career in order to care for the elderly.

One answer may be to negotiate shorter working hours – having successfully demonstrated your value to your employer, you should find yourself in a strong negotiating position.

SETTING LIFE GOALS

It is no good setting out on a journey if you do not know in which direction you should be heading.

Setting yourself life goals is essential for achieving a comfortable balance between work and home.

Practical exercise: What are your Life Goals?

Rate the following in order of importance to you at this point in your life:
I want to:

(1) Get to the top of my chosen ladder.
(2) Be well-known and successful.
(3) Earn lots of money.
(4) Gain promotion once my job no longer provides a challenge.
(5) Have a steady, enjoyable and stimulating job which does not interfere with my home life.
(6) Do routine work which I do not have to worry about, so I can give most of my attention and energy to my family.
(7) Protect my career interests so I can progress at work when my children are older.

TIPS

- Identify the major factors which are likely to prevent you from achieving your most important goal.
- Our life goals change as our life changes – review your goals every few years.

Practical exercise: Are you suffering conflict?

(1) Which do you view as most important: your career, your private life, or an even balance between the two?
(2) How often does your private life interfere with your working life? What are the major causes of the interference?
(3) How often does your working life interfere with your home life? What are the major causes of the interference?
(4) How often do you feel stressed or find your health affected by difficulties in combining your work and private life?
(5) Are your family commitments preventing you from progressing your career? Which commitments are the main cause of this?
(6) How often do you find yourself in conflict with your partner because of your work?
(7) How often do you find yourself in conflict with your partner because of your home responsibilities?
(8) What percentage of your waking time do you spend on:

   - your job
   - running the home
   - looking after your family
   - planning/working to progress your career
   - hobbies/leisure pursuits
   - physical exercise
   - resting/reading for pleasure/watching television, etc.
   - talking to your partner.

(9) If you had more time available, would you spend it on:

   - day-to-day work responsibilities
   - activities which would help you progress your career
   - day-to-day family responsibilities
   - leisure pursuits
   - general relaxation
   - talking to your partner
   - sleeping.

FAMILY-FRIENDLY WORKING PRACTICES

Values are changing for both sexes and many of us now place greater emphasis on the quality of our life as a whole, seeking more flexible working practices and increased leisure time. This plus the need to meet the requirements of working mothers and carers has given rise to the introduction of a wide range of flexible or family-friendly working practices within many organizations. The need now is to encourage *all* employers to adopt such practices as standard for both sexes at all levels.

Employers have often excluded senior positions from opportunities to work in flexible and alternative ways, which means that people who have other commitments find it hard to reach the higher ranks of their profession. The provision of more flexible work options is one method of promoting equality of opportunity. It is also an accepted means of recruiting and retaining staff and ensuring that there are no artificial barriers to the development of individuals within organisations. By offering alternative ways of working at all levels in an organisation, the pool of individuals who may be considered for management is vastly increased, thus enabling more choice for the organisation as well as individuals.

(New Ways to Work, 1993, p. 8)

The 1993 New Ways to Work Report, *Change at the Top*, was sponsored by National Westminster Bank and contains the results of a survey of over 100 people (mainly female) working flexibly at senior and managerial levels. It found that the types of senior jobs worked flexibly are extremely varied, the main reason cited for flexible working is the need for childcare with quality of life a secondary consideration, and that almost half of those surveyed worked on a job-sharing basis.

Detailed information on flexible working practices is available from a variety of sources and in particular from New Ways to Work, the educational charity whose aim is to promote flexible working arrangements. The following sections summarise the most common types of flexible arrangements.

Flexible working hours

Flexible working hours, or flexitime, is the longest-established method of flexible working other than part-time employment. Employees are contracted to work a specific number of hours in a specified timescale such as one month, can vary their working hours from day to day and take time off by working longer hours on other days. Flexitime is invaluable to the working carer who may need to take a couple of days off at short notice because of a sick child or relative. It also allows employees to travel outside the main rush hour, a boon to mothers having to travel with children.

Many companies only operate official flexitime schemes for lower-grade workers but senior workers can often negotiate an informal arrangement with their boss. Smaller organizations without an officially recognised scheme may be persuaded to agree to an informal arrangement for an individual employee.

Part-time work

This is the most common way of reducing the number of hours of work. A part-time worker is officially defined as someone who works fewer than thirty hours a week, but those who work less than sixteen hours a week have less protection under current employment legislation in respect of job security, unfair dismissal and redundancy claims. Traditionally, part-time work has only been available for low-paid, low-status workers and many employers still consider it to be impractical for supervisory and management jobs. However, an increasing number of employers are starting to make part-time work available to more senior people, for instance, Sainsbury's have introduced a new level of first-line management with an option of working part-time.

A job may be advertised as part-time or you may be able to negotiate with your employer to get your existing job reclassified. Arguments you can use to help persuade them include the retention of your skills and the cost and productivity loss they would incur should they have to recruit a new worker to replace you. If your company is looking to reduce its workforce, you could suggest that allowing you to work part-time would help them achieve this.

TIP

- Familiarise yourself with the employment and pensions legislation relating to part-time workers before deciding on the number of hours you wish to work.

Job-share

Like part-time work, job-share usually involves working a set number of hours or days, but the job itself remains classified as a full-time post and the work is shared between two or more people. Each sharer has an employment contract setting out their pro-rata pay and benefits and joint responsibility for the full-time job. The job can be divided between the sharers in a variety of ways depending upon both their own needs and those of the job.

> During the last ten years the growing use of job sharing has enabled people to work on a part time basis, without taking the drop in salary and status traditionally associated with part time work. Some companies have agreed individually negotiated job shares – an early example being that of training manager at the Stock Exchange in 1981. In late 1988 Boots Retail Division and British Telecom announced formal schemes, and since then a number of other companies, including Halifax Building Society and Prudential, have followed suit. A wide range of companies are currently looking into job sharing as one of a range of more flexible options.
>
> (New Ways to Work, 1993, p. 14)

Because partners jointly share the responsibilities and authority of the job itself it is important that they get on well with each other. Many systems include the sharers having an overlap of a few hours each week to brief each other. One advantage of job-share over part-time working is that it can easily be adapted for supervisory and management grades – because the job itself is covered full time, continuous supervision is maintained.

Term-time working

Term-time working is increasingly being adopted by companies such as Boots, B&Q, Dixons and Thistle Hotels who want to attract women back to work. Another example is the Alliance and Leicester Building Society who have a term-time working scheme for parents of children aged between five and fourteen.

Employees continue to have a permanent employment contract as either full- or part-time employees but also have the right to take unpaid leave of absence during the school holidays. They can reduce the amount of unpaid time they have off in the year by taking some of it as paid leave. Companies having a large number of their workforce on term-time working may restrict the amount of unpaid time off that each employee can take, to avoid staffing problems during school holidays.

Working from home

Homeworking, remote working or teleworking is an arrangement whereby the employee spends all or some of their time working away from the office, often at home. The homeworker remains an employee with agreed conditions of service and is not to be confused with the self-employed or contracting homeworker who works for a variety of different companies.

CPS, part of the ICL group, has operated a teleworking scheme for its staff for over twenty years and has a long waiting list of potential employees. Other companies with some form of homeworking or teleworking scheme include BP, British Gas, Grand Metropolitan, the Training Standards Advisory Service and BT. Other organizations are currently considering formal schemes or allow individual employees to work at home under informal arrangements.

One of the main reasons found for employers' reluctance to allow their staff to work from home on a regular basis is the attitude of management – homeworking necessitates management by objectives and results, whereas many managers still feel they can only be sure that their staff are working if they can see them doing so. Other reasons given for the slow take-up include the cost of equipping a home office, perceived technical/ job requirement restraints ('an employee working remotely would be unable to supervise their staff adequately') and perceived lack of employee interest. So far, homeworking has mainly been adopted by clerical staff performing routine functions or by senior management on an *ad hoc* basis. Few companies currently allow supervisory and junior to middle management staff to work from home, but there is no practical reason why homeworking, properly managed, should not be just as effective for staff at these levels.

To function effectively for both the employer and employee, homeworking schemes need to be formally managed. Without regular visits to the office, team briefings and telephone and social contact with co-workers, employees become isolated from the rest of the workforce, the company culture and potential useful career contacts and can find themselves in a career backwater. A combination of home and office working can help alleviate these problems.

Working from home is not in itself a substitute for proper childcare – as any mother who has tried to cope with a teething baby or demanding toddler whilst being chased by their employer to complete a piece of work will confirm – but used with a variety of childcare arrangements it can help provide a satisfactory balance between work and home responsibilities.

TIPS

If you think working from home would be the answer to some of your problems:

● Find out as much as you can about the schemes operated by other companies, and talk to individuals currently working or who have worked at home.

● Think carefully about the practical aspects and how you would integrate your work and home life.

● Consider how you would discharge your work responsibilities if working from home.

● Ensure you are aware of the drawbacks, including the potential problem of isolation and the effect this would have on your career prospects.

● Think about the idea from your boss's viewpoint and plan the best way to 'sell' it to them. If no formal scheme exists in your organization, suggest that you pilot the idea for an agreed period of time.

If you are currently seeking employment or looking to change your existing job, don't be deterred by the lack of advertisements for home-based working. Instead, apply for jobs in the usual way, but before the interview stage prepare your case for working from home. You may find an appropriate point in the interview to raise the suggestion, but the best time to raise it will usually be when you are actually offered the job – once the employer has decided you are the best person for them, you will be in a much stronger bargaining position.

CAREER BREAKS

In 1993 the Institute of Personnel Management (IPM) recommended that employees of both sexes should be allowed breaks of up to five years to enable them to balance work with family life, citing a number of reasons why an individual might want to take time off, including caring for children, older people or the long-term ill or disabled, to travel or to obtain additional education and qualifications. As well as helping reduce the conflict between work and home, such breaks can be used by individuals to help them widen their experience and increase their 'employability'. To support their recommendations, IPM published a very useful guide for individuals considering a career break (Institute of Personnel Management, 1993).

The most common reason for a career break is to raise children; the next most common is a sabbatical for study leave or other personal reasons. A career break may last from a few months to many years, and the effect it has on your career depends on both the length of time you are away from the workforce and your attitude to your future career.

If you intend to continue your career or take up a new one after your break, it is vital to properly plan your break beforehand. It is all too easy to concentrate on the break itself and put off thinking about your return to work until it becomes imminent, only to find that you have become out of touch with the world of work, thus adversely affecting your employment prospects and your self-confidence. The most common barriers returners to work cite are:

- lack of confidence
- lack of knowledge about current working practices
- being out of touch with people of influence in the world of work
- out-of-date skills
- lack of recent work experience
- not knowing where to start in the search for a job or new career
- under-rating the value of their personal skills and experience, including transferable skills.

TIPS

When taking a career break:

- Keep yourself fully advised of developments in the world of work during your break, by keeping in touch with your employer/former employer and working colleagues, reading company literature, business press and professional journals, and making the time to network with existing and new contacts.
- Keep your existing skills up to date and learn new ones during your break, by studying, taking training or doing voluntary or part-time work.
- Properly plan your return to work, being clear about the type of career you intend to pursue, keeping yourself informed about current developments in that field of work and obtaining or refining the skills you will need to be successful.
- If taking an extended career break, seek returner training at the end of it to identify and update your skills, boost your confidence, refresh your memory about jobsearch techniques and obtain contacts and support.

COPING WITH CONFLICT

Conflict between work and home life will adversely affect your career prospects unless you learn to resolve the conflict or cope with it. The most effective way of coping will depend on your individual circumstances and personality.

TIPS

- Be aware of the inter-relationship of your work and home life at all times and learn to recognise potential causes of conflict before they become a major problem.
- Be clear about your overall life goals and where your priorities lie.
- Learn to recognise the symptoms of stress and tackle the cause, not the effect.
- Don't bottle up problems until they cause a major crisis – seek the help and support of friends, colleagues, counsellors, mentors and employers from the outset.
- Consider your circumstances as objectively as possible – think how you would advise a friend or colleague who was in a similar situation.
- Be aware of your relationship with your partner and the effect that work or domestic problems have on this.
- Consider the benefits to be gained from flexible working and thoroughly plan your negotiations with your employer before attempting to obtain permission to adopt a different working pattern.
- Be prepared to have to make some compromises in order to achieve a comfortable balance – if you need to give priority to your children for a few years, you may have to accept that this will slow down your career.

And finally:

Do not attempt to be Superwoman. It is impossible for any of us to maintain a perfectly spotless house, look after our partner and our children *and* hold down a responsible and challenging job – if you try to do this, the only thing you will achieve is an early burn-out.

7

DISCRIMINATION, HARASSMENT AND STRESS

Sexual discrimination – Positive action – Racial distrimination –
Age – Coping with disability – Harassment – Stress

Discrimination is the unequal treatment of individuals or groups compared to other like individuals or groups. At work, discrimination may
occur because of gender, marital status, parental status, race, religion,
age, physical ability or, in fact, anything that makes an individual or
group seem different to that which is perceived as the norm. Most discrimination is illegal, but some, such as positive action for under-
represented groups, is not only legal but is actively encouraged.

Harassment occurs when an individual is subjected to unacceptable mental, verbal or physical attacks, and is in itself a form of discrimination. The
worst form of harassment suffered by women generally is of a sexual nature.

SEXUAL DISCRIMINATION

It is unlawful to treat anyone, on the grounds of sex, less favourably
than a person of the opposite sex is or would be treated in the same
circumstances.

(Equal Opportunities Commission, 1992, p. 2)

There are two kinds of discrimination: *direct* – where a woman is treated
less favourably than a man because she is a woman, and *indirect* – where
the general conditions applied to employees favour one sex more than the
other but cannot be justified. An example of indirect discrimination
would be an employer stipulating that all staff in a particular job must
meet certain physical criteria, such as a minimum height, when this criterion cannot be justified by the requirements of the job itself.

Under the Sex Discrimination Acts 1975 and 1986 (SDAs) women and
men have equal rights, and sex discrimination in advertising, recruitment, training, promotion, rates of pay, general treatment at work and
dismissal is illegal. Equal rights also apply to married people, who must
not be treated less favourably than single people.

Recruitment

Job advertisements must not state or imply a preference for male or female applicants or for single or married people, and must not include criteria which would bar one or other sex from applying, if these criteria are not an essential part of the job. Recruitment and headhunting agencies, jobcentres and careers offices are also covered by the SDAs and cannot restrict the field of candidates to one or other sex unless a person's sex is a genuine occupational qualification for that particular job (the Acts fully specify the circumstances in which Genuine Occupational Qualifications (GOQs) are permitted).

All job applicants must be considered as individuals, not as a man or a woman, and a job offer must not be made to someone simply because they are the same sex as the people with whom they will be working or because the company wishes to increase the number of employees of that particular sex. The only exceptions are for jobs where a specific sex is required, for instance to preserve decency and privacy – in such cases, it will be necessary for the employer to formally claim exemption and demonstrate that the exemption claim is legally valid under the SDAs.

Selection testing

Selection tests used in recruitment and promotion must not discriminate against either sex. Tests must not be designed in such a way that a man would find them easier than a woman, and vice versa. Individual questions should have no sex bias – for instance, questions of a technical nature should not use examples or terminology with which a man would be more familiar than a woman, unless the examples related specifically to the job content.

Training

Training must be made available equally to both sexes on equal terms and must not be denied to an individual because of their sex. A training course held at times or a location which would make it difficult for a woman or a part-timer to attend would be deemed to be discriminatory unless an alternative, such as distance learning, was offered. Employers should not assume that a woman would not want to be offered training because of her sex.

Promotion

As in recruitment, employers must treat both sexes equally and offer the job to the best person – it is unlawful for them to discriminate against an employee because of their sex, marital or parental status. Employers must not assume that a woman could not do the job because of her family responsibilities, nor must they assume that a woman would not want to do the job because in the past it has always been done by a man.

Employers need to be aware of management practices and individual attitudes which may discriminate against women. Failure by individual managers to appraise women or put them forward for promotion, because the manager feels a woman would not want to do a higher-grade job or might not be capable of doing it because of her sex, constitutes sex discrimination.

General conditions of service

Again, both sexes must be treated equally. Special privileges such as time off to care for a sick child or the facility to job-share must not be given to a woman unless a man would also be given this privilege, if requested. Maternity leave is the only exception to this.

Dismissal, redundancy and retirement

Again, both sexes must be treated equally. Since 7 November 1987 it has been unlawful for employers to compulsorily retire a woman at State Retirement Age for women if a man doing the same or similar job would be allowed to work until age 65.

Discrimination on marital grounds

Direct discrimination occurs when a married person is treated less favourably than a single person of the same sex would be treated in similar circumstances. Indirect discrimination occurs when a requirement or condition has the effect in practice of disadvantaging a higher proportion of married people than it would single people. For example, if an employer stipulated that job applicants had to be able to travel or work unsocial hours when in practice this would never be required, this could disqualify or discourage married people from applying for the job and would therefore be unlawful.

Equal pay

Under the Equal Pay Act 1970 (as amended 1983), an employee is entitled to pay and other contractual terms and conditions equal to that received by employees of the opposite sex if they are doing work which is the same or similar, or has been rated as equivalent by an analytical job evaluation scheme or if the work they do is equal in terms of the demands made on the worker. Differences in pay and conditions are only allowed if there is some material difference between the jobs as done by a man or a woman, or if there is some other difference not connected with sex which justifies the difference in pay, such as London weighting payments to employees of both sexes working in a specific geographic location.

Case study

Allison Ogden, Director of Women's Education in Building (WEB), moved to her present job after encountering what she deemed to be discrimination by her previous employer, the Union of Construction, Allied Trades and Technicians (UCATT). Allison worked for UCATT as Assistant Research Officer responsible for equal opportunities issues, where in the past the Assistant had been promoted to Head of the Research Department when that post fell vacant.

After being Assistant for two years, Allison began to think about opportunities for promotion and when the Head of the Research Department told her he planned to move on to another job, Allison felt she had a good chance of being offered promotion. However, her real ambition was to become a National Officer dealing with health and safety, issues which she feels are very important in the construction industry. As a National Officer, she would have political influence and a much higher profile and would be in a position to be able to use the power this would give her to help further the interests of UCATT members. Although Allison had the necessary qualifications and experience plus substantial support from colleagues, at this time there was no full-time National Officer for Health and Safety, nor had a woman ever been appointed as National Officer. Coincidentally, she found herself being headhunted by WEB.

Allison approached the General Secretary of UCATT, told him about the offer from WEB and said that although the new offer was for higher pay, she would be happy to remain with UCATT if he could confirm that he would support her bid for becoming a full-time National Officer. Although he said he felt she would have been very good at such a job and he would have liked to create the post, he told her that he 'didn't feel the union was ready for a woman as a National Officer'.

Allison had previously encountered a hostile attitude from the General Secretary, and her opinion is that the over-riding reason for him not wanting to create the post she proposed was because she is female, although his attitude might also have been influenced by the fact that additional power being associated with health and safety could have made the union unpopular with the construction industry.

Although she was furious about his attitude and had good contacts within UCATT who would have supported her, she weighed up all her options and decided that fighting the case was not the right answer, given that in the senior post she would have had to work very closely with the General Secretary who could have made things very difficult and stressful for her, had she been appointed against his express wishes. She was also in the fortunate position of having another job offer, which she decided to accept.

Allison has gone on public record as being critical about both UCATT's attitude to women generally and what she deems to be prejudice in the Tracie Simpson harassment case. She is a fighter who is always willing to stand up for women and does not easily give in – 'I am all in favour of women being trouble-makers' – but feels that in her own case, even if she had fought and won, the drawbacks would have outweighed the benefits, particularly as in her view, one of the biggest problems to be overcome is that until the desire to change is there, it is very difficult for individuals to force change.

Discrimination against mothers

Women taking maternity leave have a statutory right to return to work after the birth of their child provided they meet certain criteria (as laid down in the Employment Protection (Consolidation) Act 1978). This includes the right to be allowed to return to the same job if this is reasonably practicable, or to a similar job, and the right not to be dismissed 'for pregnancy or any other reason connected with pregnancy'.

An employee of either sex with parental or caring responsibilities must be treated equally to a childless employee. However, if parental or caring responsibilities prevent the employee from fully discharging all their work responsibilities in an acceptable way, the employer may be able to claim that the employee's work is below standard and thus take action against them under general employment law.

Handling sex discrimination

Any person who feels that they have been unlawfully discriminated against in employment is entitled to take action. The increasing number of women taking formal action and the increased publicity given to sex discrimination cases go a long way towards encouraging other women to fight their cases, and also make employers more aware of discrimination and more wary of the possibility of legal action should they act unlawfully. Despite this, sex discrimination, particularly indirect, still abounds – including cases such as a woman being sacked because she wore trousers to work.

What has made a huge difference (in the USA) is women willing to go to court, fight, stand up and be seen, and gain awards which hit the employer in the pocket.

(A Californian woman visiting the UK)

You need not be an employee to claim sex discrimination – individuals who feel that an employer's recruitment and selection procedures are discriminatory are also entitled to take action.

If you suspect you have been discriminated against on the grounds of sex, you should:

- ascertain your rights, by contacting the Equal Opportunities Commission (EOC) and/or the Advisory, Conciliation and Arbitration Service (ACAS) – these organizations provide a whole range of free booklets relating to sex discrimination
- collect as much 'hard' evidence as possible, including written statements from witnesses and others involved. Keep written notes about the occurrence and copies of all relevant correspondence
- seek professional advice and help from your trade union, professional association and/or the EOC and ACAS, and moral support from family, friends and colleagues
- take the complaint up in the first instance with the employer, requesting them to state the reason for the treatment which gave rise to your complaint. You can do this either by letter or by using a Sex Discrimination Act questionnaire form SD 74 (available from the EOC, trade unions, professional associations, local employment office, jobcentre or unemployment benefit office). The employer is not legally bound to reply to your request, but failure to do so, or an evasive or ambiguous reply, may go against them at an industrial tribunal hearing
- if you do not receive a satisfactory explanation, call in a conciliation officer from ACAS or take the complaint to an industrial tribunal. Details about tribunals are given in a free leaflet *Industrial Tribunals Procedure*, available from jobcentres, employment offices and unemployment benefit offices
- ensure that you take formal action within the maximum time period allowed. A complaint under the SDAs *must* be presented to the industrial tribunal no later than one day less than three months after the perceived discrimination occurred.

TIP

- Before deciding to take action, think carefully about the effect on you as an individual:

    - it is likely to involve you in a great deal of work and stress and possibly expense
    - fighting a case, particularly in court, can be traumatic – the tribunal will look into your work record in detail
    - even if you win your case, you could end up in an uncomfortable position at work where relationships with your employer are strained
    - you are likely to be disappointed with the level of compensation you win.

However, failure to fight your case may result in the employer continuing to discriminate against women and may also leave you with feelings of guilt. The more we use the law to fight for the rights due to us, the more likely employers are to treat women fairly.

Victimisation

This occurs when an employee of either sex is treated less favourably than other employees are or would be treated, because they have complained about, or support people who have complained about, discrimination. Victimisation is unlawful, therefore an employer must not discipline or dismiss an employee on account of their complaint.

Obtaining help from the EOC

The EOC provides help and advice about sex discrimination and equal pay. They give free general advice, advice on how to make a complaint, and will sometimes provide formal assistance in taking a complaint to a court or tribunal. Formal help is limited to those cases where a difficult point of law is involved, a case is so complicated that it would be unfair for the individual to deal with it by themselves, or where a complainant's position in the organization or relationship with the individual they are complaining about makes it inappropriate for them to handle their own case.

POSITIVE ACTION

Positive discrimination is unlawful, but if people in a particular group, such as women, have been under-represented in a particular area of work or geographic location for the previous twelve months, employers are permitted to take positive action to redress the situation.

Positive action in recruitment advertisements is permitted under section 48 of the SDA, allowing employers to encourage job applications from women or men for jobs which either sex would be capable of doing, in order to increase the number of that particular sex in that field of work. Although employers are permitted to encourage one or other sex to *apply* for a specific job, they are not allowed to discriminate against applicants on the grounds of sex when selecting which of them to appoint. Also, employers are not permitted to use this facility to operate a quota system.

Positive action can be used to encourage under-represented groups such as women to apply for particular jobs or for jobs in a specific geographic location, by ensuring that the wording and media used for advertising those jobs is 'woman-friendly' so that women are not put off from applying because they feel that a woman could not do the job or would not be welcomed in it.

Positive action training

Section 47 of the SDA permits positive action in training and education, where action is needed to attain equality of opportunity in the workplace. Positive action training to help a specific group of people learn how to handle a selection test is permitted, provided the test is relevant to a specific job. Positive action training for selection testing generally is not permitted.

If women require additional skills so as to be able to apply for a wider range of jobs or for jobs at a specific level, single-sex training is permissible in order to maximise the potential of that group of employees. Positive action may be used to encourage women to apply for training, to make access to courses more readily available, and to provide single-sex training courses where there is a requirement for this. Training may include courses to develop the trainees' confidence and assertiveness where these skills are needed by women in order to be able to do a particular job; skills updating; training in a particular technique such as supervision or interviewing; career counselling and guidance; mentoring; or to provide new skills in areas where there is a skills shortage, either within a particular company or in a specific geographic location. The onus is on the employer to prove the requirement for positive action training – it is not enough for them just to assume there is a need for this.

Reasons used by employers for not appointing women to particular jobs include the argument that women do not show any interest in applying for the job or for training. Investigations by the EOC have found that women are often put off from applying because of the way that job or training is described – if the industrial/practical side is stressed, women are less likely to apply whereas if emphasis is put on the people/caring side or on the benefits the applicant would gain, women are more likely to apply.

Positive action in recruitment and training should preferably be part of a total positive action programme rather than an isolated initiative. There is little value in appointing women to jobs or training them for promotion if other barriers, such as company attitudes, job shortages, lack of childcare facilities or family-friendly working practices, etc. are not also demolished.

TIPS

If you are offered positive action training:

- be aware of the possible attitudes of individual colleagues and be prepared to have to 'smooth their ruffled feathers'
- ask your employer what additional support or opportunities will be available to you after the programme.
- be realistic about your expectations – your career prospects are unlikely to improve dramatically overnight.
- use the training to develop support networks as well as improve your skills or learn new ones. Keep in regular contact with your support network after the training.

If not carefully handled, positive action may in itself create barriers for women. Men may resent and feel threatened by what they deem to be special treatment, women colleagues not offered access may also feel resentful. Women on a positive action programme may feel threatened if they think their relationships with colleagues could be adversely affected. Women may have their expectations raised, only to be let down through lack of continued company support or job opportunities.

RACIAL DISCRIMINATION

The Race Relations Act 1976 makes it unlawful to discriminate against a person, directly or indirectly, in the field of employment.
(Commission for Racial Equality, 1991, p. 7)

'Racial grounds' are described as the grounds of race, colour, nationality – including citizenship – or ethnic or national origins. As with the Sex Discrimination Acts, racial discrimination in recruitment, selection, terms of employment, training, promotion, discipline and dismissal is unlawful; however, positive action to help under-represented racial groups is permitted, and selection on racial grounds is allowed for specific jobs where being of a particular racial group is a genuine occupational qualification.

Where an employee has particular cultural and religious needs, such as traditions of dress for Asian women or the observance of prayer times and religious holidays, which conflict with their work requirements, the Commission for Racial Equality's (CRE's) Code of Practice recommends that employers should consider whether it is reasonably practicable to adapt the job requirements to enable the employee to meet such needs.

The Race Relations Act applies to individual employees and trade unions as well as to the employer – discrimination or victimisation of one employee by another or by a trade union on grounds of race is unlawful.

Indirect discrimination can arise from working practices or attitudes which disproportionately disadvantage members of a particular racial group. Often, such discrimination is not intended, but arises because the employer has not considered the effect traditional practices might have on different racial groups – for example, an employer who recruits mainly through word of mouth via existing employees, where information about vacancies would be unlikely to reach different racial groups if few or no members were already employed by that company.

Handling racial discrimination

If you feel you have been discriminated against, either directly or indirectly, on racial grounds, contact the CRE in the first instance to ascertain your legal rights. As for sex discrimination, take the matter up in the first instance with the perpetrator; if the discrimination continues, take legal action.

> **TIP**
>
> ● It is very easy to unintentionally discriminate against someone of a different race or cultural background through not properly understanding their outlook and requirements, i.e. by judging that person by our own standards and assuming that their outlook is the same as ours. We should each examine our own behaviour to ensure that we are not guilty of prejudice or unintentional discrimination.

AGE

Unlike sex or race discrimination, age discrimination is not unlawful in the UK and is frequently shown overtly. There are no legal regulations to prevent employers from advertising jobs with an upper or lower age limit, although such practice is publicly deplored by professional associations, etc.

Studies show that employers tend to associate particular characteristics with age. Responsibility, reliability, work commitment and a desire to remain with an employer are expected to increase with age whereas ambition, flexibility and adaption to change, trainability, mobility and willingness to travel or work unsocial hours and willingness to use new technology are expected to decline. Older workers are perceived to be better suited to jobs requiring low skill, low responsibility and repetition and to be unsuited to physically demanding, time-consuming or IT-based jobs. Many employers are reluctant to recruit older workers because their skills are not fully up to date and they feel that older people are more likely to be set in their ways, have inflexible attitudes and are beginning to fail physically.

However, there is no hard evidence to support these assumptions, and some companies, such as B&Q, actively recruit older workers and have found these initiatives very successful.

The public sector is more likely to recruit older people and provide flexible working practices. Older women workers are predominantly employed in clerical and personal services, and in professional and managerial occupations, with over 50 per cent of them working part time. Older men tend to be found in professional and managerial occupations and over 90 per cent work full-time.

Age discrimination can occur in recruitment, selection, training, promotion and redundancy. Employers may use age criteria to short-list applicants – even if this is not an overt decision, their assumptions about older workers' unwillingness to travel or work unsocial hours may preclude people over a certain age being short-listed. They may be reluctant to offer training to older workers – reasons cited include:

– insufficient time to get a return on the investment

- older people cannot or do not want to learn new skills
- older workers have sufficient experience and do not require further formal training
- older workers need general management expertise and do not require technical skills
- older workers are unlikely to want or be suitable for promotion and therefore do not require training.

Obviously, such generalisations cannot be justified. There are numerous examples of people in their fifties and sixties demonstrating ambition, seeking new challenges, learning new skills and making good use of training to enhance their management experience. Studies show that the ability to solve problems and acquire, understand and manipulate new information remains constant or increases with age. Improved health and living conditions mean that people are physically and mentally active for longer.

The government-backed Carnegie Inquiry, the result of a three-year, £1-million project, highlights the rising age of the working population and the need for employers to use older people to supplement the dwindling workforce. It calls for a radical change in approach by government and employers to allow people to work into their seventies if they wish, provide more flexible pension schemes, laws to end age discrimination unless objectively justified, and promotion of work for older people. However, until age discrimination becomes unlawful, stereotyping, and to a certain extent the attitudes of older people themselves, will continue to perpetuate age discrimination.

Women suffer from age stereotyping more then men, being perceived generally to be less ambitious and to have reached their peak at an earlier age. Older women are also perceived as being less qualified than men because of maternity breaks and as having more time-consuming family commitments, whereas in reality a woman's family commitments are likely to decline with age as her children become older and more self-reliant.

Barriers created by individuals

Individual older workers, as with women generally, are in danger of creating their own barriers which help perpetuate discrimination. Barriers include:

- assuming they are 'past it' when they reach a specific age
- assumptions that employers are looking only for younger people to recruit or promote
- fear of being shown up by younger people
- fear of failure, being less willing to take risks
- fear of being too old to learn.

Handling age discrimination

If you suspect you have been discriminated against because of your age, consider whether a man in your position would have received the same treatment – you may be able to take action under the sex discrimination or equal pay legislation. If the company claims to be an Equal Opportunities Employer, point out to them that age discrimination runs directly counter to the spirit of equal opportunity practices.

TIPS

- be aware of your own self-image and ensure that you are not creating your own barriers or reinforcing others' attitudes about older people
- take every opportunity to update your skills and acquire new ones, and let others know that you are doing so
- actively let your employer know that you are keen to undertake training or advance your career
- stress to employers the benefits they would gain from your age and experience, and point out the pitfalls of making generalised assumptions based on stereotyping – younger people can be just as, or more, set in their ways than an older person
- whatever your age, consider omitting it from your CV. If enough of us adopt this practice, employers may eventually stop using age as a criterion by which to short-list applicants
- actively seek opportunities to undertake new challenges and publicise your successes
- seek out role models and successful older women to cite as examples to employers
- campaign for a change in employer attitudes and for legislation to end age discrimination.

COPING WITH A DISABILITY

I thought ACCESS was a form of credit card until I discovered steps.

Under The Disabled Persons (Employment) Acts 1944 and 1953 all employers with twenty or more workers must employ a quota of registered disabled people (currently 3 per cent of their workforce) and must not, without reasonable cause, dismiss a registered disabled person or employ anyone who is not registered disabled, if they have not met their quota. However, employers below quota can apply for a permit to employ non-disabled people if there are no suitable registered disabled people available. In addition, under the Companies Act 1985, all large companies must include in their annual report a statement of their policy on the employment of disabled people.

In practice, few employers actually achieve the legal quota, though if it can be shown that in recruitment an employer is discriminating against disabled people they can be refused a permit to employ non-registered people.

Few individuals with no form of disability properly understand the needs of disabled people. We take for granted our ability to handle stairs, the telephone, computers, meetings and travel. The most common reaction when faced with a disability is to treat that person as 'different' or to assume that they are unable to carry out certain tasks – many people are unable to treat a disabled person as an equal. This arises more from unfamiliarity and fear of causing offence than from active prejudice. It often shows itself as over-sympathetic or protective behaviour ('I think you are so brave') or appears patronising.

Case study

Sue Hancock, Women's Equality Advisor for the London Borough of Waltham Forest, has been blind from an early age. She received special schooling from the age of 4 and by the time she was 10 years old she felt that her community regarded her as inferior and did not want her. She was told that there would be very few jobs open to her and even at university was told that she would never be able to make a living in the fields of work which interested her – the only professions she was recommended to pursue were secretarial work or physiotherapy. She blames her early problems on the fact that she was sent to a special school, where the segregation from the rest of the community outweighed the benefits of specialist teaching.

Sue has brought up two children, coped with divorce, and has a successful career, initially in teaching, including teaching English in Sweden as a second language, and then in equal opportunities issues. She has had to face comments and interview questions such as 'How will you go to the toilet/make the coffee/keep discipline in the classroom/get to work?'. Rather than treating her blindness as a handicap, she has worked hard to turn it into a benefit and to help other disabled women do the same.

> Being blind has given me a unique set of skills I can use which sighted people do not have. I have learned to deal with the problems society hands me, and to become aware of issues and see them from other people's point of view.

Sue advises disabled women to:

- value yourself; recognise the need to convince yourself of your importance and value, don't be apologetic – you are not an inferior person
- believe that disabled people have a lot to give, and concentrate on identifying the talents such as negotiating and being creative that you have developed in order to cope with the discrimination

you have had to face. Translate these into work terms and sell them as an asset
- don't treat disability as a medical condition or a personal defect. Remind yourself that it is society which imposes the problems – 'It's not my wheelchair which keeps me out of the building, it's the steps'.

She recommends that employers need to:

- recognise that by not employing women and/or disabled people they are missing out on having the use of unique talents
- look at how their employment practices discriminate or exclude disabled women, such as using standard job application forms which ask whether the applicant has a current driving licence when the particular job does not actually involve having to drive
- when recruiting or promoting, ask themselves what the person *must* be able to do in order to carry out their responsibilities satisfactorily, as opposed to what it would be nice for them to be able to do or what previous postholders have been able to do. Think *when* the job needs to be done (i.e. during what hours), *where* it needs to be done (location), *how* it needs to be done and *why*. Have an open mind and look for innovative/creative solutions rather than insisting on traditional working practices merely because they are traditional
- do not assume that a disabled person would prefer to work from their home – most prefer to get out and mix with society rather than being cut off from it.

In summary, Sue feels that if society were better adapted, fewer people would be excluded, there would be less prejudice arising from a lack of understanding, and employers would have access to a wider range of skills and talent.

Fears faced by disabled women include:

- being asked/expected to do something beyond their capability
- feeling that their job security or promotion prospects are threatened
- fear of harassment if they cannot perform to normally expected standards
- being blamed for a department's poor sick record.

Tips given by other disabled women include:

- ensure that you are fully aware of your employment rights
- accept that your energy may be diminished, and learn the best way to cope with this
- believe that you have the right to say no if something is beyond you
- believe in your right to have time off work for medical reasons – do not let yourself feel guilty
- teach yourself to ask people to help/support you

TIPS for non-disabled women

- Remember that disabled people are people first and disabled second. The term 'the disabled' is viewed by people with disabilities as demeaning.
- Make an effort to understand the needs of disabled people and help them, in the most appropriate way, to fight discrimination and harassment and to achieve their full potential. As a start to understanding, read up on publications aimed at disabled people – the Royal Association for Disability and Rehabilitation (RADAR) produce a very good booklet.
- Ensure that all your staff actively understand the needs of people with disabilities.
- When organising seminars, conferences, meetings, etc., find out whether any delegates have any special needs. Hold the event in a location with access for disabled people, provide a sign language interpreter and induction loop for the hard of hearing, etc., as required.

- make the most of your existing skills and constantly seek to learn new skills/become multiskilled.

HARASSMENT

Harassment occurs when a person is treated in a detrimental way on improper grounds. It can take many forms and may be directed at an individual or group of individuals. Sexual harassment is defined in the EC Code as 'unwanted conduct of a sexual nature, or other conduct based on sex, affecting the dignity of women and men at work'. Individuals may also experience harassment because of their race, sexual orientation, religion, political convictions, trade union affiliation or non-membership, disabilities, age or youth, status as ex-offenders, their real or suspected infection with AIDS/HIV, or other grounds. In fact anyone who is perceived as being different may be vulnerable. Harassment can be either overt, such as an unwanted sexual approach, or covert, such as failing to keep a person informed about matters of interest to them. It may be instigated by an individual or arise from company policy such as allowing the display of sexually offensive posters or calendars. Harassment is a form of bullying, and is often carried out by individuals who themselves feel insecure and who feel the need to demonstrate their power over others.

Some individuals may actively invite harassment by making a point of flaunting their differences in unacceptable ways, or may perceive harassment when none has been intended. Genuine harassment is often difficult to prove and individuals may feel vulnerable or embarrassed and be reluctant to complain about it.

Harassment constitutes discrimination under the Sex Discrimination, Race Relations and Fair Employment Acts. The European Commission has adopted a Recommendation on the protection of the dignity of individuals at work and a Code of Practice on measures to combat sexual harassment. A Statement based on the key principles in the EC Code of Practice is available free of charge from the IPM.

Sexual harassment

Sexual harassment ranges from disrespectful or offensive behaviour towards women generally, through derogatory remarks about an individual or women in general, to uninvited and unwelcome overtures from male colleagues or, at the extreme, to full-blown sexual attacks. Women may be more vulnerable when their colleagues are mainly male or when their job entails working late or travelling with male colleagues. Socialising with male colleagues after work can also make us vulnerable; single women may be more at risk than married women. Some women find themselves being faced with blackmail where senior male colleagues intimate that the woman's failure to accept their approaches will adversely affect their career (the 'casting director's couch').

Some of us may unintentionally invite sexual approaches:

> When my marriage broke up my husband's departure left me feeling unwanted and unloved and I desperately needed reassurance that I was still liked as a person. My boss became very attentive – without realising it I had been giving off signals of wanting male attention. Fortunately I realised what was happening in time to call a halt before things went too far.

The effect of harassment

Harassment causes humiliation, stress, trauma and often health problems for the victim, adversely affects their work performance and in severe cases may force them to resign from their job. It can destroy their self-confidence – constant devaluing of the victim's work performance leads to them feeling devalued as a person and may destroy their personal life and that of their family. Some victims long for vengeance and seek retaliation, which creates additional problems.

Harassment creates problems for the employer because of poor employee morale and loss of productivity, and it is in the employer's interests to ensure that harassment does not occur or is quickly stamped out and that the company has a clear policy on harassment and how this is handled. Employers have a legal responsibility to take appropriate measures to ensure that their employees do not suffer any form of harassment. However, many companies still have no formal policy on sexual harassment.

Dealing with harassment

If you feel you are a victim of any form of harassment or bullying:

– consider first whether the perpetrator intended to harass you. It may be that a remark you found offensive would not be seen as such by

another woman and that the individual did not realise they were causing offence. Also, consider whether your own actions may have unintentionally helped to create the situation
- ensure you know your rights and obligations. Ask yourself whether the demands made of you are reasonable within the terms of your employment contract and job description. Find out whether your employer has a written policy on harassment and familiarise yourself with their formal grievance procedures
- attempt to resolve the problem informally with the individual concerned, by telling them the effect their behaviour had on you and asking them not to repeat it. If you feel unhappy about facing them on your own, ask a friend or union/professional association representative to be present when you speak to them
- if you or your work are constantly criticised, request a specific explanation about what you are doing wrong and what you need to do to improve
- take action as soon as possible. Turning a blind eye will not make the problem go away – letting the harasser get away with their behaviour will only encourage them to continue acting that way, will reduce your self-esteem and make it more difficult for you to tackle the perpetrator
- if colleagues are also suffering harassment from the same source, seek their support in taking action
- if the harassment continues, fully record all occurrences, unpleasant remarks or unfair criticism and if possible get colleagues to witness these or provide supporting evidence. Talk to either your manager, your Personnel Department or the manager of the perpetrator and request their help
- if informal requests fail, make a formal complaint to your employer and seek help/guidance from your trade union/professional association or from the Citizens Advice Bureau or the EOC
- a final resort is to seek legal action on the grounds of sexual discrimination, unfair or constructive dismissal and through criminal law on assault
- if you suffer stress, trauma and ill health because of the harassment, seek immediate counselling or medical help.

STRESS

Pressure is a part of our everyday life. It is the sum of the demands put upon us, and without demands we are unlikely to achieve much. Not all pressure causes stress, but an excess of pressure beyond a level with which we can comfortably cope causes us to feel stressed. Conversely, a lack of pressure such as being in a boring job with no challenge and where we feel undervalued can also cause stress. The capacity to cope

---

TIPS: Coping with harassment

● Do not put up with behaviour which you find unacceptable, merely because your colleagues do not object to that behaviour.
● Do not be frightened of taking action merely because the perpetrator is senior to you. You have the right to be treated with respect and in a fair way – do not accept anything less than this.
● Take action immediately the offence occurs – bottling your reactions up and brooding on the offence will do you no good.
● Be aware of your own behaviour towards others – are you inviting sexual or racial, etc. comments; do you make such comments to others which they might find offensive; are you ever guilty of behaving in a bullying or harassing way to others?

---

with pressure varies from person to person; what one person views as a challenge creates stress for another. Our personal coping level varies from time to time – demands we take in our stride one day may cause us stress the next, particularly if we are feeling under par physically that day.

Recognising stress

Stress in humans originally arose from being faced with a physical danger. The body reacted to the danger by releasing adrenalin and preparing to 'fight or take flight'. Although most stressful situations today are caused by mental rather than physical threats, the body reacts in the same way. Typical symptoms include:

– tense shoulders and neck
– dilated pupils
– dry mouth
– increased heart rate and blood pressure
– sweating
– upset stomach
– being over-emotional and bursting into tears, particularly if someone offers us sympathy
– exaggerating the situation out of all proportion
– becoming obsessed with our problem
– becoming aggressive/defensive, feeling that everyone is out to attack us
– losing our temper over the smallest thing
– feeling guilty when relaxing
– insomnia
– difficulty in concentrating
– difficulty in making decisions
– feeling frustrated
– drinking or smoking to excess.

Prolonged stress causes severe mental and physical problems such as blurred vision, headaches, dizziness, breathing difficulties, backache, high blood pressure and palpitations and skin disorders.

Recent studies in Australia seem to indicate that men and women may react differently to stress due to differences in the chemistry of male and female brain structures. Males are seen to become aggressive under stress whereas females become defensive.

Some people are more prone to stress than others, particularly those known in medical circles as coronary-prone behaviour pattern Type A people – those of us who are highly competitive, impatient, hard-working with a lot of drive, enjoy a challenge, hyper-alert, restless, etc., as opposed to the Type B personality – calm, relaxed and easy-going, patient, less competitive and ambitious. Few people are totally one type or another; we all exhibit a mixture of both characteristics and can modify our behaviour when required.

Causes of stress

Stress may be caused by a specific situation or person, by a number of situations combined or by 'free-floating anxiety' – background worries which never seem to leave you. Typical causes of stress in working women include:

- lacking confidence or feeling self-conscious
- feeling isolated, an outsider, not 'belonging'
- dealing with people in authority
- being criticised or perceiving criticism
- being treated unfairly
- having to fight for our rights
- not feeling in control of a situation/lacking the authority to take control or take action
- fear of failure
- fear of the unknown
- feeling undervalued
- career barriers
- harassment
- worrying about what others think of us
- the pressures of balancing work and home responsibilities
- taking on too many responsibilities because we feel unable to say no.

Lack of challenge or pressure is a commonly overlooked cause of stress. Being in a job where we are operating below our capacity may put pressure on us to do something about it, but also leads to lethargy and a feeling of 'can't be bothered', where making an effort to change the situation becomes too much trouble. Although we may not consciously feel stressed, we will feel generally dissatisfied with life – this adversely affects our general physical and mental well-being just as much as being under too much pressure. Unemployed people are a prime example of this – often lacking a sense of purpose or having difficulty in motivating themselves to continue their jobsearch campaign.

Practical exercise – Identifying stress

List up:

(1)   Your physical reactions to stress.
(2)   The type of situations which make you feel stressed.
(3)   Identify your specific stress 'triggers' – are there any particular patterns in the causes you have identified? Do you feel more stressed when your health is not 100 per cent? Are your triggers predominantly work- or home-based?
(4)   Identify what you perceive to be the difference between pressure and stress.

Coping with stress

We are all capable of building up our resilience so that fewer situations cause us stress, and also of increasing our capacity to cope so that we avoid serious physical and mental damage when we do encounter stressful situations.

TIPS

- Learn to recognise when you are feeling stressed, by getting to know and understand your physical and mental reactions, thus learning to identify the symptoms at the outset and take early action to prevent them becoming chronic.
- Take action to avoid the most common causes if at all possible or to minimise the frequency of occurrences.
- Analyse the stressful situation as objectively as possible – often when we do this we find that the threat is not as bad as we thought or it may even turn out to be non-existent.
- You may not immediately be able to identify the cause of your stress, particularly if there are a number of, possibly unconnected, contributing factors. If you feel generally unhappy, picture yourself in an ideal situation and then try to identify which factors of your actual situation, or which people, are missing from the picture – these are likely to be the ones which are contributing to your stress.
- Take steps to reduce the effect the stress has on you:

  – re-assess your own abilities and judgements. Concentrate on your strengths and successes to put yourself in a more positive frame of mind and increase your coping abilities
  – when you feel threatened and under stress, your ability to behave assertively is impaired. Practise being assertive in everything you do, not just in connection with the stressful situation itself

---

- practise reducing your hostility towards others by taking a deep breath and stopping to think before confronting them
- identify and concentrate on all the positive aspects of the situation
- release the build-up of adrenalin by taking stamina-building rhythmic physical exercise such as strenuous walking, jogging, cycling or swimming. The exercise must be enjoyable and relaxing – avoid competitive exercise which will increase your stress
- use relaxation techniques such as yoga and meditation to dispel muscular tension and reduce your breathing and heart rate
- remind yourself that work is not everything. Set aside time to spend in places/situations/with people where you feel safe, relaxed and tranquil. Make a positive effort to relax and switch off from your worries
- cut down on alcohol and smoking – they may help you unwind temporarily but in the long run will create additional problems
- talk yourself into a calmer frame of mind. Remind yourself that there is no such person as Superwoman and that you have the right to be less than perfect. Stop trying to drive yourself too hard/do everything at once/please everybody.

- Take action to remove the stress by resolving the situation which is causing it. If the situation continues:
  - seek official help in resolving it. It is not in your employer's interests to have you continue to be stressed – your work performance will be impaired, you may make serious mistakes and health problems may affect your productivity.
  - seek professional medical help. Talk to your GP in the first instance but don't just ask them to treat your physical symptoms – tell them what you think the cause is. If necessary, they will refer you to a specialist who will help you cope until the cause is removed.

- If your stress is caused by too little, rather than too much, pressure in your job, look for other ways to find a challenge, such as taking up a competitive sport, a new hobby or academic or vocational study. The feeling of well-being you gain from this will provide the impetus you need to take action to change your work situation.

Helping others who are stressed

A good manager learns to spot stress in their staff and colleagues and takes steps to help them resolve their problems or at the least to avoid putting them under additional pressure. Be alert for the physical symptoms of stress; a suddenly deteriorating work performance may also be an indicator.

Remember that they may not themselves realise that they feel stressed, or that it may be a personal problem which they would prefer not to discuss with you. Be sympathetic and let them know you are happy to help if they want you to. You may have to reduce their workload or responsibilities – be very careful how you do this; if they think you lack confidence in their abilities, this will increase, not reduce, their stress. Beware of trying to 'jolly them out of it' – this may be the last thing they want. Treat them in the way you would yourself like to be treated under similar circumstances.

I suffered prolonged stress through frustrations at not being able to progress my career. My colleagues took a bracing, rather than sympathetic, attitude – they told me to accept the situation instead of fighting it, saying it was an unfair world. They may have been right in the long run, but what I most needed at the time was both a shoulder to cry on and confirmation that I did have ability and was being treated unfairly. As it was, I ended up doubting my own judgement of my ability, and gave up the fight.

Finally, ensure your staff are not feeling stressed because of too little pressure; i.e. because they lack stimulating work or are not being used to their full ability.

8

THE WAY FORWARD

Career backwaters – Finding your direction – Setting your goals – Seeking out opportunities – Turning your failures into success – Training

My ambition grows as I grow – I will probably never get to where I want to be because my goal is constantly changing.

Although many successful women openly admit to never having actively planned their career, few of us today are likely to progress much further unless we consciously think about where we want to get to and plan the best way to get there.

CAREER BACKWATERS

We need to believe in what we are doing and know that we are doing something important and worthwhile. Commitment, involvement, dedication and excitement all provide a sense of achievement. Without challenge, there is little sense of achievement – this happens when we become stuck in a career backwater or are heading in no particular direction.

Practical exercise: Are you in a career backwater?

(1) How long have you been in your present job?
(2) How frequently do you feel bored or frustrated with it?
(3) Does the thought of staying in it for the foreseeable future make you feel depressed?
(4) Is your performance less good than it could be? How much have you allowed your standards to slip because you have lost interest or don't need to think about what you are doing?
(5) Do you take more days off sick for minor ailments than you used to?
(6) Do other people's jobs seem more interesting than your own?
(7) Do you feel envy or a sense of unfairness when you hear of friends or colleagues getting a better job?
(8) Is your job a defined stepping stone on your career path?

(9) How much opportunity does it give you to develop your existing skills, learn new ones, tackle new challenges, take on increased responsibility and make use of your full potential?

Other symptoms include becoming irritable, lacking patience with others, a feeling that you are too good for the job and that your skills are being wasted, an increasing belief that your colleagues are incompetent, feeling that you are being treated unfairly and your skills are overlooked or are being deliberately ignored.

Recognising that you are in a backwater is one thing – doing something about it is much harder. Change involves effort and is a risk – it is much easier to succumb to inertia, refuse to admit that you need a change and find excuses not to move on. Yet outstaying your welcome in a job is extremely damaging both to your career prospects and to yourself as an individual.

Typical excuses given for not making an effort to change:

- I expect to be offered promotion some time in the future
- I need to finish my current project before I can think seriously about the future
- I need a little more experience at this level
- I don't have time to look for new opportunities
- it would be disloyal to my employers to think about leaving them
- the employment market is so uncertain right now that I can't afford the financial risk of changing jobs
- it would be difficult to learn a new job as well as cope with my family commitments
- there are so many people with more experience and better qualifications than me looking for jobs – I wouldn't stand much of a chance
- if I got a more demanding job I might not be able to do it as well as I thought I could.

Taking risks

If you don't try, you can't fail.

Remaining in a stagnant career is an even greater risk – the longer you stay there, the less chance you have to learn new skills and gain new achievements, and the less attractive you will seem to a new employer. Not taking risks means you have no opportunity to achieve anything, which itself constitutes failure. The more you attempt, the easier it becomes to overcome a fear of failure and the greater your chances of success.

Taking positive action to manage your career is not a major risk. By planning where you want to get to, analysing your best options and taking the route most likely to succeed, the likelihood of failing is less than if you merely react to circumstances.

It is much easier (and more comfortable in the short term) *not* to plan your career. Thinking about yourself and your capabilities involves self-analysis – you sometimes discover things about yourself that you do not like.

TIPS

- Identify all the positive benefits to be gained from properly planning your career.
- Consider carrying out the exercise with a friend or group of friends or going to a professionally run career seminar (many women's networks run these).
- Set yourself a specific deadline by which you are going to make a start on planning.

FINDING YOUR DIRECTION

You wouldn't set off on a journey without knowing where you intended to end up and planning how you were going to get there.

A career is not just a succession of different jobs, it is a journey in a specific direction which heads towards a specific destination. Setting goals gives meaning and purpose to life and achieving those goals provides a sense of personal fulfilment. The average person continually functions well below their capability and underachieves their potential, often because they undervalue themselves and their abilities. You owe it to yourself to make the effort to continually seek challenge and opportunities for greater achievement.

Practical exercise: Defining success

In a few short sentences, define what you consider constitutes success in your career. Ensure that this fits comfortably with your overall life goals.

TIPS

- Success provides peace of mind and freedom from fear, stress and guilt; a feeling of dynamic health and energy; quality relationships with the people around you; freedom from financial worry; and a sense of personal fulfilment. It allows you to live your life to the full and get the maximum amount of enjoyment out of all you do. Achieving success enables you to look back on your life and be able to say 'Yes, my life has been worthwhile, and will continue to be so'.
- Your definition of success, and thus your overall goal, will change as you and your career change and develop.
- Success attracts others to you; the way you view and present yourself affects the way they think about you.

Two men were seen working in a quarry. When asked what they were doing, one said 'I'm chipping away at granite'; the other said 'I'm helping to build a cathedral'.

Success does not come easily – it involves honest (and often traumatic) self-analysis, systematic planning, hard work and sustained effort. It means taking risks and inevitably involves some failures and setbacks along the way.

Deciding on the right direction

However well you think you know what you want from your career, you will still benefit from reminding yourself about the basics and clearly defining in writing the direction you plan to take. There are numerous good books available on career planning; I have merely listed below a few tips to bear in mind. Once you have made the decision to actively plan your future career path you can read up further on the subject or take professional advice.

TIPS

- Write a pen-picture of your ideal job and compare this with your definition of success and your overall life goals.
- Re-read the summary of career barriers in Chapter 1 and identify all the barriers currently preventing you from achieving your ideal job. Decide what action you will take to demolish or by-pass the barriers.
- Identify all your personal qualities and achievements, skills, experience and qualifications, plus your personal interests and transferable skills. Get a good friend, close colleague or your mentor to list up what *they* feel are your qualities, skills, achievements, etc. They are bound to find some you missed because you discounted their value or took them for granted.
- Compare the qualities and experience needed for your ideal job with your own attributes, and list up the action you are going to take to fill the gaps.

By now, you should have a fairly clear idea of your career aspirations and can start planning the best way to achieve these.

SETTING YOUR GOALS

A goal is a dream with a deadline.

Success is the continued achievement of predetermined, worthwhile goals.

Without defined goals or objectives you have nothing by which to monitor your progress and you will lose your sense of direction. Having identified where you wish to end up, the next stage is to set yourself specific objectives. Your objectives should be:

- written down, so they don't get forgotten
- specific rather than vague, so you can monitor your progress
- realistic and achievable
- staged, so you don't tackle too much in one go and aren't overwhelmed
- set against a specific timeframe, with a date by which you are going to achieve each of them
- regularly monitored and reviewed, and amended as needed.

TIP

- Having identified your objectives, visualise yourself having already achieved each of them in turn, utilising the scenario concept – develop a brief narrative describing the new characteristics of your career as it will be at that stage. Write your narrative as if the objective has already been achieved. i.e. 'I am . . .' – avoid using words like 'will', 'could', 'might'.

SEEKING OUT OPPORTUNITIES

Career guidance

The range of work-types is huge – around 10,000 occupational titles have been identified in the UK alone – and jobs with a similar-sounding title may differ widely in content and responsibility level. Thus, career guidance cannot be an exact science but it does help to eliminate totally unsuitable careers.

TIPS

- Visit your local Careers Office for general information plus pointers to other sources of assistance.
- Talk to your friends and business contacts to find out what their jobs involve.
- Consider taking an aptitude test or psychometric interest inventory or seeking professional counselling from career or outplacement consultants.

Finding job opportunities

Consider opportunities open to you or which you can create within your own company. Are your managers fully aware that you want promotion or a career development move? Are your talents fully visible? Are you demonstrating that you have what it takes? It is not enough just to want to get on – you need to market yourself just as actively as if you were seeking work with a new employer.

TIPS

- Be alert (but not oversensitive) to the possibility that you may be missing out on opportunities within your organization because of:

  - managerial assumptions that, as a woman, you would not wish promotion or are not capable of it
  - lack of contacts which prevents you hearing about forthcoming opportunities
  - inflexible managerial attitudes which assume that higher-level work can only be done in the traditional working way, thus indirectly discriminating against women with caring responsibilities or a disability.

- Don't wait for posts to become vacant. Create an opening by suggesting innovative ways in which your skills could be put to good use or highlighting the need for new projects.

It's not what you know, it's who you know.

Many jobs are never advertised publicly but are offered to people already known to the employer, either because their achievements are highly visible or because they are recommended by someone whose judgement the employer trusts. Other jobs go to people who have approached a prospective employer on the off-chance that they might at some stage have a suitable position for them (the speculative approach).

TIP

- Put at least 70 per cent of your effort into a combination of networking and speculative approaches rather than concentrating on answering job advertisements.

Applying for jobs

As in any marketing campaign, the more closely you target your approach, the more chance of success. Applying for jobs takes time and money; sending out hundreds of applications may only generate hundreds of rejection slips.

Headhunting

There is a certain amount of mystique surrounding headhunting and much status falsely attached to being headhunted. An individual usually becomes aware that they are being headhunted only when they get an unexpected telephone call and are asked about their career and plans. The

---

TIPS: Applying for jobs

- Concentrate on seeking out those employers and jobs which most closely match your ideal and on cultivating useful contacts, researching the employer's needs and tailoring your application to clearly demonstrate that you meet those needs. In short, sell yourself to them.

- Fully research the company before applying:

  - is its culture and structure one with which you would feel comfortable?
  - does the job form a positive step forward on your career path, providing challenge and an opportunity for learning new skills, gaining new achievements?
  - do you know any contacts who can put a good word in for you?
  - what new initiatives is the company taking that you can refer to in your covering letter, to demonstrate your interest in them?

- Take a close look at your CV:

  - is it up to date?
  - does it clearly describe *what* you are, *what* you have achieved and the benefits you can offer a potential employer?
  - does it contain 'skills stories' to illustrate your achievements?
  - is it professionally produced on top-quality paper and does both its content and its visual appearance have immediate impact on the reader? (Remember that selectors look at each application for no more than thirty seconds when initially shortlisting)
  - do you amend it to be specific to each particular job for which you apply?

---

natural reaction is to feel that you, as an individual, have been singled out by a new employer, but this is not usually the case.

Headhunting companies work on behalf of employers, who provide a precise brief describing the position to be filled and the required attributes. The headhunter identifies positions in other companies likely to have posts filled by someone suitable – for instance, if the vacancy is for a Financial Director in a large plc, the headhunter will look for a similar post in a smaller plc or a Financial Manager post in the same size company. Having identified companies with such positions, the headhunter will find out (often from the switchboard operator) the name of the person currently occupying that post. In most cases, the headhunter knows nothing in advance about that person – thus people who are headhunted are contacted because of the *job* they currently have, not because their personal achievements and qualities are known to the headhunter.

TURNING YOUR FAILURES INTO SUCCESS

If you believe you can, you will; if you believe you can't, you won't.

Every failure has a positive side to it. The trick is to identify and build on the positive points so that you turn your failure into a future success.

Make a note of your performance as soon as you come out of a job interview. Request feedback each time you are not selected, and identify those things which you will do better in the future. Consider each failure as an opportunity to improve your chance of success next time.

Practical exercise: Turning failure into success

List up all your failures over the past few years. For each of them, identify at least one positive aspect or lesson you have learned and how you will use these to become successful in the future.

TRAINING

Employment Department statistics show that, overall, employed women receive less training than men. In general, training is concentrated on younger people; young men are more likely to get training than young women but this is reversed for the older age groups, probably because of the training available to women returning to work.

There are several reasons why women receive less training than men, including:

- employer attitudes which assume that women do not need or want training, therefore do not offer them training opportunities
- courses held at times or locations inaccessible to women with family responsibilities or who work part-time
- women failing to request training.

Regular training and skills updating for all employees is essential in today's employment market. Employers need to be aware of the likely areas of future skills shortages and train their existing workforce to provide these skills. Training opportunities and formal training plans help improve employee morale as well as their skills. Regrettably, many employees still report receiving less training than they would like.

Greater emphasis is being given to vocational, rather than academic, skills, and initiatives such as Investors in People are being run to encourage employers to train their staff and provide them with opportunities to gain NVQs. Pressure is being put on training providers to make their courses more relevant to employment and to provide customised training in those areas where skills will be needed in the future. Alternative means of study such as open and flexible learning mean that there are no longer grounds for employers refusing to train women who are unable to attend full-time courses.

The responsibility for ensuring adequate training provision cannot be left solely to the employer. To be successful, we must each take personal responsibility for ensuring that we receive the training we require to progress our career. This is particularly relevant if you have been with your current employer for some time and have progressed by promotion without gaining additional formal qualifications. Instead of the 'job for life' outlook of previous decades, today's employment scene is one of employees regularly moving between different companies – if your formal qualifications are low, you may find difficulty in getting yourself shortlisted for interview.

TIPS

- Regularly review your training needs. Concentrate on those areas which will help you advance your career within your required timescales.
- Familiarise yourself with the awards available to you under the NVQ system (contact the National Council for Vocational Qualifications) and the Investors in People Initiative (contact your local TEC).
- Familiarise yourself with the alternative methods of training, such as open and flexible learning.
- Ask your employer to provide the training you require, pointing out the benefits they will gain from this. If they cannot provide the training themselves, ask if they will pay your fees to attend an external course. If they refuse, investigate further to see whether you are being discriminated against.
- If your employer cannot meet your requirements, find out what training is available from your professional association, trade union or women's network.
- If you are between jobs, request details of free training and career development loans from your local jobcentre or TEC.
- Ensure you provide your staff with the training they need – ideally, draw up a personal career and training plan for each of them and regularly review this with them.

Training requires commitment, time, and (sometimes) finance, which are not easy to find whilst holding down a full-time job. However, if lack of training is holding up your career progression, your only alternative may be to accept that you will go no further. The choice is yours!

9

CONCLUSIONS

Action for the employer – Action for the individual – Conclusion – Reflection

Some glass ceilings are beginning to be shattered or at least cracked. Equal opportunities is now on political and board agendas and the message that this makes good economic sense as well as being about justice, fairness and people is beginning to get home.

(Joanna Foster)

There is no doubt that women face far more career barriers than do men. But some of these are partly of our own making and, whatever the cause, there is always some positive action we can take to surmount or by-pass them. It is up to each of us as an individual to take responsibility for our own life and not only take the positive action needed to break through our own personal glass ceiling, but also help other women to do the same.

ACTION FOR THE EMPLOYER

The most important employer initiative to occur during this decade is Business in the Community's Opportunity 2000 campaign, launched in October 1991. By July 1993 200 employer organizations had become members, committing themselves to 'increasing the quality and quantity of women's participation in the workforce by the year 2000'. Priority action areas identified by employers include cultural change, the appointment and retention of senior women, and family-friendly working practices. The campaign continues to grow, with the progress of member organizations monitored against set goals and additional employers being actively encouraged to join the campaign.

Almost as important is the government's Investors in People campaign, launched in November 1990 with the objective of improving training standards within firms and encouraging the development of a 'training culture within organisations'. Aimed at companies employing 200 or more people, the campaign seeks to gain commitment to the campaign by 50 per cent of all such companies by 1996. Because women receive less training overall than men, this campaign must help increase our opportunities, though the impact may be reduced because the campaign is limited to larger employers and women are more likely than men to be employed by smaller organizations.

Such initiatives can only be successful if all organizations, however large or small, take part. Employers will only ensure their future effectiveness and profitability by taking action now to look to that future and put the required working practices and culture in place so that they attract and retain the best possible employees. All employers need to:

- ascertain the number and levels of women currently employed by them and the barriers their female employees face
- analyse their existing working practices and cultures
- initiate a change of culture throughout the company to dispel existing stereotyping and prejudices
- introduce family-friendly working practices for both sexes
- initiate formal career planning and training programmes for all employees
- introduce a written equal opportunities policy and ensure that the spirit, as well as the letter, of this is maintained throughout the company.

TIPS

- Actively encourage your employer, either individually or via your professional association or trade union or a women's network, to join the Opportunity 2000 campaign and find out more about Investors in People.
- At the very least, actively encourage your employer to introduce a formal equal opportunities policy.

ACTION FOR THE INDIVIDUAL

We can no longer carry on with women having to adapt to men's culture. We have to get in there and change the culture so that it equally suits women.

(Trudy Coe, Institute of Management)

Challenge the existing structure – think how you can help create a culture which allows equal opportunity for all.

Although we have all individually achieved what we have in our lives, these are not individual achievements – we need to acknowledge those who fight for the freedoms which allow us to achieve.

(Sumita Dutta, Director, SIA)

The glass ceiling is created by outdated government, trade union, employer and individual attitudes and prejudices towards women. But we must, to some extent, hold ourselves responsible for allowing it to continue. It is useless to complain about the unfairness if we do not also take responsibility for finding ways of making the best of our own personal situation. The glass ceiling exists – that is a fact of life. What we must each do is to find the best way of breaking through it, and then take positive action to remove the causes once and for all.

One of the most positive findings to come out of my research for this book was the large numbers of women I found who actively help and support other women. As well as giving advice and assistance on a personal level to individual women that they know, a great many volunteer to stand up and talk about their experiences at public seminars, where their tips and encouragement provide us with the incentive to go out and do as well ourselves.

TIPS

- Don't allow yourself to become isolated – many other women share or have experienced your problems. Make an active effort to talk to others to gain their advice and support.
- Don't keep your achievements to yourself. Sharing these with other women will help them break through their own glass ceiling as well as providing you with wide publicity for your abilities.
- Work with other women in both formal and informal groups to help change the traditional working culture.
- Don't assume that the traditional promotion routes are the only ones – seek out innovative ways to get through or around your own personal barriers.

CONCLUSION

The phenomenon of the glass ceiling is now widely acknowledged not only by individuals but by employers, professional associations, trade unions and the government. Many positive initiatives are under way and although it may take years yet to completely demolish all the barriers, moves in the right direction are definitely being made. By continuing to fight against second-class treatment, we will eventually succeed in achieving our rights.

I hope this book has provided you with the understanding you need to break through your own glass ceiling. The next step is up to you.

REFLECTION

If you think you are beaten you are;
If you think that you dare not you don't.
If you'd like to win, but think you can't
It's almost certain you won't.

If you think you'll lose you've lost.
For out in the world you'll find
Success begins with a woman's will –
It's all in the state of mind.

If you think you are outclassed you are.
You've got to think high to rise;
You've got to be sure of yourself before
You can ever will a prize.

Life's battles don't always go
To the strongest or fastest one.
But sooner or later the woman who wins
Is the one who thinks she can.

Anon

APPENDIX: PERSONALITY TRAITS QUESTIONNAIRE

Tick the ten words that most closely describe you, and put crosses against the ten words which are least like you.

Patient	Moderate
Assertive	Open-minded
Trusting	Sociable
Eager	Diplomatic
Decisive	Restless
Confident	Submissive
Respectful	Sensitive
Friendly	Conventional
Accurate	Obedient
Energetic	Cautious
Persistent	Receptive
Timid	Precise
Cheerful	Optimistic
Animated	Stubborn
Intellectual	Practical
Pessimistic	Logical
Imaginative	Creative
Artful	Outspoken
Independent	Peaceful
Modest	Well-organised
Competitive	Self-motivated
Emotional	A loner
Helpful	Changeable
A leader	Reticent
Aggressive	Sensible
Tenacious	Speculative

After making your choices, cover your markings and get someone who knows you well to choose the words they think best describe you, then compare their view to your own markings.

REFERENCES

Commission for Racial Equality (1991) *Race Relations Code of Practice.*
Davidson, M.J. and Cooper C. L. (1992) *Shattering the Glass Ceiling – The Woman Manager* Paul Chapman Publishing, London.
Employment Department, *Labour Market Quarterly Report,* Employment Department, Moorfoot, Sheffield.
Employment Department (1992) Skills and Enterprise Update, May, referring to *Supervision (Advisory Booklet number 17),* ACAS.
Equal Opportunities Commission (1992) *A Short Guide to the Sex Discrimination Acts,* free leaflet.
Henley Management College (1992) *Clerical and Secretarial Skills,* (and annotated bibliography) available from Greenlands, Henley-on-Thames, Oxfordshire RG9 3AU.
Hepburn, P. (1991) *Checklist for Action, Secretaries: Still a Wasted Asset?,* The Industrial Society.
Hewitt, P. (1993) *About Time – The Revolution in Work and Life,* IPPR/Rivers Oram Press, London.
Institute of Personnel Management (1993) *Employment Breaks – an information pack for personnel professionals considering a voluntary break from employment.*
The Institute of Personnel Management, *Statement of Harassment at Work,* free leaflet.
New Ways to Work (1993) *Change at the Top – Working flexibly at senior and managerial levels in organisations.*
The Royal Association for Disability and Rehabilitation (RADAR), *Into Work – A Guide for People with Disabilities,* free booklet.
Spencer Stuart & Associates Ltd (1993) *Point of View No. 17, Women in Management,* available from 16 Connaught Place, London W2 2ED, free booklet.

FURTHER INFORMATION

Childcare

Black and Ethnic Minority Childcare Working Group
Wesley House
4 Wild Court
London WC2B 5AU

Childcare Umbrella
c/o 77 Holloway Road
London N7 8JZ
tel: 071–700 5771

Daycare Trust
Wesley House
4 Wild Court
London WC2B 5AU
tel: 071–405 5617/8

Kids' Club Network
279–281 Whitechapel Road
London E1 1BY
tel: 071–247 3009

National Childminding Association
8 Masons Hill
Bromley
Kent BR2 9EY
tel: 081–464 6164

National Council for One Parent Families
255 Kentish Town Road
London NW5 2LX
tel: 071–267 1361

Pre-School Playgroups Association
61–63 Kings Cross Road
London WC1X 9LL
tel: 071–933 0991

Working Mothers' Association
77 Holloway Road
London N7 8JZ
tel: 071–700 5771

Flexible working/family-friendly working practices

New Ways to Work
309 Upper Street
London N1 2TY
tel 071–226 4026

Flexible Working for Managers by Isobel Boyer, available from Teresa Walter, Publishing Sales Department, CIMA, 63 Portland Place, London W1N 4AB, tel: 071–637 2311, £12.95 + £2.00 p&p.

General reading

Barriers to Fair Selection by David Collinson, HMSO, £6.50.

Best Companies for Women by Scarlett MacGwire, 1992, Pandora Press, £7.99.

Bullying at Work by Andrea Adams, Virago, £6.99.

Career Planning by Marilyn Davidson, available from Wyvern Business Library, £3.95 + p&p.

The Century Gap by Harriet Harman, 1993, Vermillion, £7.99.

Confident Conversation by Dr Lillian Glass, 1991, available from Wyvern Business Library, £14.99 + p&p.

Corporate Culture and Caring: The business case for family friendly provision, Institute of Personnel Management, available from Business in the Community, £5.00.

Coping with Difficult Bosses by Robert Bramson, 1993, available from Wyvern Business Library, £16.99 + p&p.

Developing your Style by Susie Faux, available from Wyvern Business Library £12.95 +p&p

The Glass Ceiling Breakers (video) available from Wilcox Bulmer Productions Ltd, 12 Cambridge Court, 210 Shepherds Bush Road, London W6 7NL, £19.80.

The Influential Woman by Lee Bryce, available from Wyvern Business Library, £10.95 + p&p.

The Key to the Men's Club: Opening the doors to women in management by Trudy Coe, IM Books, Burston Distribution Services, Newbridge Close, Bristol, £30 (£15 for IM members).

Life, Work and Livelihood in The Third Age, The Carnegie UK Trust, available from Bailey Management Services, 127 Sandgate Road, Folkestone, Kent, CT20 2BL, £19.50.

Networking and Mentoring – A Woman's Guide by Dr Lily M Segerman-Peck, Piatkus.

Play to your Strengths by Donald O. Clifton and Paula Nelson, 1993, available from Wyvern Business Library £15.00 + p&p.

Sexual Harassment in the Workplace available from ISCO, 5, The Paddock, Frizinghall, Bradford, BD9 4HD.

Stress That Motivates by Dru Scott, 1993, available from Wyvern Business
Library, £14.95 + p&p.
Successfully Ever After by Shirley Sloan Fader with Penny Kane, 1985, Piatkus,
£7.95.
The Power of Persuasion by Rupert Eales-White, 1992, available from Wyvern
Business Library, £19.95 + p&p.
Which Way Now? – How to plan and develop a successful career by Bridget A.
Wright, 1992, Piatkus, £8.99.
Women as Managers (fortnightly news-sheet), available from The Economics
Press (UK) Ltd, Berkley House, Barnet Road, London Colney, St Albans,
Herts, AL2 1BR, tel: freephone 0800 515815, £58.50 for one year's
subscription.

Homeworking and self-employment

National Homeworking Unit
3rd Floor
Wolverley House
19 Digbeth Street
Birmingham, B5 6BJ
tel: 021–643 6352

OwnBase (The National Association of Home-based Workers)
68 First Avenue
Bush Hill Park
Enfield
Middlesex EN1 1BN
tel: 081–363 0808

Women into Business
Small Business Bureau Ltd
46 Westminster Palace Gardens
Artillery Row
London SW1P 1RR
tel: 071–976 7262/3

Home is Where the Office Is by Andrew Bibby, 1991, Hodder & Stoughton,
£6.99.

Personality and psychometric testing

The British Psychological Society
St Andrews House
48 Princess Road East
Leicester LE1 7DR
tel: 0533 549568

Liburtum
Ash Business Centre
Ash House
Ash Road
New Ash Green
Kent DA3 8JD
tel: 0474 879494

Psychological Testing for Managers by Dr Stephanie Jones, 1993, available from
Wyvern Business Library, £18.00 + p&p.

Teleworking

Alan Denbigh
ACRE
The Other Cottage
Shortwood
Nailsworth
Gloucestershire GL6 0SH
tel: 045 383 4874

Telecottage Association
WREN Telecottage
Stoneleigh Park
Warwickshire CV8 2RR
tel: 0203 696986

Telework: The human resource implications by John and Celia Stanworth, avail-
able from the Institute of Personnel Management, £12.95 + £1.20 p&p.
Teleworking: a strategic guide for management by Steven Burch, 1991, Kogan
Page, £18.95.
Training for Teleworking available from the National Council for Educational
Technology, Sir William Lyons Road, Science Park, Coventry, CV4 7EZ,
£3.50.

Training

Catalyst (formerly Women and Training)
Hewmar House
120 London Road
Gloucester, GL1 3PL
tel: 0452 309330
(provides information on training and development for women.)

The National Council for Vocational Qualifications
222 Euston Road
London NW1 2BZ
tel: 071–387 9898

National Council of Industry Training Organisations
5 George Lane
Royston
Herts SG8 9AR
tel: 0763 247285

Open College
Freepost
Warrington WA2 7BR

The Open University
Central Enquiry Service
PO Box 200
Milton Keynes MK7 6YZ

Get Qualifications for What You Know and Can Do by S. Simosko, 1992, available from Wyvern Business Library, £14.95 + p&p.

Useful addresses

Advisory, Conciliation and Arbitration Service (ACAS)
27 Wilton Street
London SW1X 7AZ
tel: 071–210 3000

Business in the Community
227A City Road
London EC1V 1LX
tel: 071–253 3716

Commission for Racial Equality (CRE)
Elliot House
10–12 Allington Street
London SW1E 5EH
tel: 071–828 7022

Equal Opportunities Commission
Overseas House
Quay Street
Manchester M3 3HN
tel: 061–833 9244

The Industrial Society
Robert Hyde House
48 Bryanston Square
London W1H 7LN
tel: 071–262 2401
(Contact the Pepperell Unit for advice on training and career development for women.)

Institute of Administrative Management
40 Chatsworth Parade
Petts Wood
Orpington
Kent BR5 1RW
tel: 0689 875555

Institute of Directors
116 Pall Mall
London SW1Y 5ED
tel: 071–839 1233

Institute of Management
2 Savoy Court
The Strand
London WC2R 0EZ
tel: 071–497 0580

Institute of Personnel Management
IPM House
Camp Road
Wimbledon
London SW19 4UX
tel: 081–946 9100

Public Appointments Unit
Cabinet Office
Horse Guards Road
London SW1P 3AL

The Prowess Register Ltd
118 Eaton Square
London SW1W 9AF

The Royal Association for Disability and Rehabilitation (RADAR)
25 Mortimer Street
London W1N 8AB
tel: 071–637 5400

Wyvern Business Library
Wyvern House
6 The Business Park
Ely
Cambs CB7 4JW
tel: 0353 665544

Voluntary work

The National Council for Voluntary Organisations (NCVO)
Regent's Wharf
8 All Saints Street
London N1 9RL
tel: 071–713 6161

Women's organisations and networks

300 Group
36–37 Charterhouse Square
London EC1M 6EA
tel: 071–600 2390

The Bloomsbury Club
c/o Susan Harrison
38 Welbeck Street
London W1M 7HF
tel/fax: 071–252 0665
(Business centre and club for woman.)

British Association of Women Entrepreneurs
33 Caithness Road
London W14 0JA
tel: 071–602 4656

British Federation of University Women
Crosby Hall
Cheyne Walk
London SW3 5BA
tel: 071–352 5354

City of London Business and Professional Women
23 Ansdell Street
London W8 5BN
tel: 081–673 1215/071–938 1729

The Fawcett Society
46 Harleyford Road
London SE11 5AY
tel: 071–587 1287

National Alliance of Women's Organisations
279–281 Whitechapel Road
London E1 1BY
tel: 071–247 7052

National Council of Women
36 Danbury Street
Islington
London N1 8JU
tel: 071–354 2395

Skills and Enterprise Network
Employment Department
Moorfoot
Sheffield S1 4PQ
tel: 0742–594598

The Royal Society of Arts
Women's Advisory Group
8 John Adam Street
London WC2N 6EZ
tel: 071–930 5115

UK Federation of Business & Professional Women
23 Ansdell Street
London W8 5BN
tel: 071–938 1729

The Women Returners' Network
2nd Floor
8 John Adam Street
London WC2N 6EZ
tel: 071–839 8188

Women At Work Network
c/o Equality Exchange
Equal Opportunities Commission
tel: 061–833 9244

Women In Management
64 Marryatt Road
Wimbledon
London SW19 5BN
tel: 081–944 6332

Women's National Commission
Secretariat
Caxton House
Tothill Street
London SW1H 9NF
tel: 071–273 5486

INDEX